Refire: A Roadmap for Teachers to Rediscover Purpose and Joy in Retirement

Copyright © 2025 by Dr. Cynthia Barnett. All rights reserved.

Legal Notice:
All Rights Reserved. No part of this book may be used, reproduced, duplicated, or transmitted in any manner whatsoever without the expressed written permission of the author. You do not have resale rights or giveaway rights to this book. Only customers who have purchased this book are allowed to view it. If you believe you have an illegal copy or know someone who does, please email us at Drcynthiabarnett@gmail.com.

Disclaimer Notice:
Please note the information contained within this document is for educational and entertainment purposes only. All effort has been executed to present accurate, up-to-date, reliable, and complete information. No warranties of any kind are declared or implied. Readers acknowledge the author is not engaged in the rendering of legal, financial, medical, or professional advice. This book's content has been derived from various sources. Please consult a licensed professional before attempting any techniques outlined in this book.

By reading this document, the reader agrees that under no circumstances is the author responsible for any losses, direct or indirect, that are incurred as a result of the use of the information contained within this document, including, but not limited to, errors, omissions, or inaccuracies.

Published by:
Aviva Publishing
Lake Placid, NY
(518) 523-1320
www.AvivaPubs.com

ISBN: 978-1-63618-381-7 (softcover)
E-Book: 978-1-63618-383-1
Library of Congress Control Number: 2025904562
Editor: Tyler Tichelaar, Superior Book Productions
Cover Design & Interior Book Layout: So & So
Back Cover Photographer: Alaric Campbell

Rave Reviews for

Refire: A Roadmap for Teachers to Rediscover Purpose and Joy in Retirement

"As we get older, many of us know what we want out of life, but few of us have learned how to get it. Refire: A Roadmap for Teachers to Rediscover Joy and Purpose in Retirement gives you the roadmap to help you create a happier, more fulfilled, and meaningful life in simple and easy steps."

— David Riklan, Founder of SelfGrowth.com, The #1 Self-Improvement Site on the Internet

"An important book for anyone who wants to live a more fulfilled life in retirement! It outlines powerful strategies that would help you create the life you desire and deserve."

— Stephanie R. Ko, Author of Trading Your Way to Wealth

"Brilliant! Here is a toolkit for anyone who wants to have a joy-filled, meaningful retirement. The techniques and strategies will help you go further and set you on a path toward greater happiness and success."

— Terri Levine, The Guru of Coaching

"Cynthia Barnett holds the key to getting you excited about retirement. Let's face it—playing golf or watching soaps all day will get old fast. Instead, this book will reignite your past passions and prepare you for the next great adventure in your life. Refire: A Roadmap for Teachers to Rediscover Joy and Purpose in Retirement is the perfect gift for anyone over fifty who wants their life's next phase to be the best phase."

— Tyler R. Tichelaar, PhD and Award-Winning Author of The Mysteries of Marquette

"Just as a graduation is a commencement and not a termination, so this book teaches you how to make your life into a series of beginnings. I call it being born again, and no matter what your age, with a little labor on your part, it is possible. So let Dr. Cynthia be your midwife to a new life."

— *Bernie Siegel, MD, Author of 365 Prescriptions for the Soul and 101 Exercises for the Soul*

"For anyone who is planning to retire or has retired aimlessly, this book is a must. Even those who think they had a workable plan for retirement will find that the exercises and introspective reviews will provide added focus and clarity for a more meaningful "Refirement." I developed strategies for addressing my shortcomings and actually began implementing the action necessary to improve."

— *James Nixon, Stamford, Connecticut*

"This book has been wonderful for me. It has given me the power to make a plan and stick with it. Also to realize how strong I really am! I am going to work on my goals, clean up clutter, and plan for the future."

— *Nancy Jullian, Baltimore, Maryland*

"Happiness, fulfillment, and meaningful retirement can be yours! Refire: A Roadmap for Teachers to Rediscover Joy and Purpose in Retirement will help you take your life to the next level and achieve your deepest-held dreams."

— *Prill Boyle, Author of Defying Gravity: A Celebration of Late-Blooming Women*

"If you are looking for the blueprint of a happy, meaningful, and fulfilled retirement, look no further than Refire: A Roadmap for Teachers to Rediscover Joy and Purpose in Retirement."

— *Jeff Keller, Bestselling Author of Attitude Is Everything*

"As a retired teacher, Refire: A Roadmap for Teachers to Rediscover Joy and Purpose in Retirement has been a game-changer for me. Dr. Cynthia Barnett's blend of practical advice and inspirational stories propelled me to start writing the book I've always dreamed of. This book is more than just a guide—it's a catalyst for transformation, helping retirees like myself reclaim their zest for life and carve out meaningful, joyous paths forward in our golden years."

— *Janet Stewart, Retired Culinary Arts Instructor*

"Refire: A Roadmap for Teachers to Rediscover Joy and Purpose in Retirement is an inspirational, practical, and important read. Filled with captivating reinvention stories and hands-on exercises, this book provides a customizable roadmap for anyone approaching retirement. I highly recommend it!"

—*Nancy Collamer, Retirement Coach, Founder of MyLifeStyleCareer.com, and Author of Second-Act Careers*

"In Refire: A Roadmap for Teachers to Rediscover Joy and Purpose in Retirement, Dr. Cynthia shares wonderful personal and professional insights combined with stories to help teachers and others find joy and purpose in this next stage of life! As you read, you'll discover her refire approach for your own retirement journey!"

—*Dr. Dorian Mintzer, Co-Author of The Couple's Retirement Puzzle: 10 Must-Have Conversations for Creating an Amazing New Life Together*

"Refire is a must-read for educators who are ready to embrace retirement as a time of renewal, not retreat. Dr. Cynthia Barnett beautifully captures the essence of what it means to transition from the classroom to a life filled with passion, purpose, and joy. With wisdom, relatable stories, and practical strategies, she guides teachers through the emotional aspects of this shift, helping them reimagine their next chapter with excitement and confidence. If you're a teacher wondering what's next, this book is the roadmap you need to make retirement the most fulfilling phase of your life."

— *Marianne Oehser, MM, CPRC, Author of Your Happiness Portfolio for Retirement: It's Not About the Money*

"As a former superintendent with more than five decades in education, I have witnessed countless educators grapple with the transition into retirement, often struggling to find renewed purpose beyond the classroom. Refire: A Roadmap for Teachers to Rediscover Purpose and Joy in Retirement is an invaluable guide that addresses this very challenge. The book offers practical strategies and heartfelt insights, empowering educators to embrace retirement not as an end, but as a vibrant new beginning filled with opportunities for growth, connection, and fulfillment. It's a must-read for any teacher seeking to transform their post-career years into a period of joy and meaningful engagement. Dr. Barnett is the perfect person to write this book, having successfully transitioned from school district administration and community service to a fulfilling career in entrepreneurship and life coaching. She's a true example of how to create a joyful and purpose-driven retirement!"

— *Dr. John Ramos*

Refire

A ROADMAP FOR TEACHERS

TO REDISCOVER PURPOSE
AND JOY IN RETIREMENT

DR. CYNTHIA BARNETT

Dedication

To the educators who have spent their lives shaping minds and inspiring futures, this is your moment to rediscover that you are meant for more. To those who refuse to settle, who believe the best is yet to come, and who are ready to make this next chapter the most rewarding, joyful, and purposeful of their lives.

To the lifelong learners who embrace new possibilities, seize opportunities, and boldly take action to refire and reimagine their future. Retirement is not the end of your story—it's the beginning of a new adventure, one where your wisdom, passion, and purpose can shine brighter than ever before.

May this book inspire you to step into this next phase with confidence and excitement, knowing that your greatest contributions, adventures, and joys still await. Here's to creating a chapter that not only honors the incredible work you've done but also celebrates the limitless potential of what's to come."

CONTENTS

Dear Teachers: Your Next Chapter Awaits 13
Introduction: Is This the Right Book for You? 14
Marching Toward My Next Chapter: The Birth of Refire 15
The Refire Mission: Rediscovering Purpose and Joy in Retirement 17
Refire Your Life: Embracing the Fullness of Retirement 18
Living With Purpose and Joy: A Call to Educators 19

Step 1 Shift Gears 22

Redefining Identity in Retirement 23
Shift Gears: Redefining Your Purpose as an Educator in Retirement 23
Consequences of Not Shifting Gears 24
Rediscovering Your Values: A Guide for Educators to Thrive in Retirement 25
What's Next for You? Shifting Gears to a Life of Purpose and Adventure 29
What's Next for You? Shifting Gears from Career to Purpose-Driven Impact 31
What's Next for You? Turning Passion into Purpose 35
Summary 36
Journaling Reflections 37

Step 2 Find Your Purpose 39

Discovering Your Purpose 39
Redefining Purpose: A New Chapter for Educators 40
Work With Purpose: A Guide for Educators in Retirement 40
Determining Your Goals: A Guide for Educators in Retirement 41
Finding Purpose Beyond Retirement: How I Refired My Life Through Amazing Girls Science 43
What's Next for You? 48
What's Next for You? Turning Experience into Impact 50
What's Next for You? Embracing New Passions and Possibilities 52

What's Next for You? Turning Passion
into Your Next Chapter — 55
Summary — 55
Journaling Reflections — 57

Step 3 Discover and Live from Your Strengths — 59

Discovering and Living From Your Strengths — 59
Discovering and Embracing Your Strengths — 60
Our Strengths Are Our Gifts — 61
Strength Discovery Exercises — 61
What's Next for You? Charting a New Course with Your Strengths — 64
What's Next for You? Answering the Call
to a New Purpose — 66
Summary — 69
Journaling Reflections — 71

Step 4 Manage Your Time Effectively — 73

Effective Time Management — 73
Time Management and Purpose — 74
Lifelong Learning: Mastering Time Management in Retirement for Teachers — 74
How to Make an Activity Log — 75
Why Keep an Activity Log? — 76
How to Keep an Activity Log — 77
Learning from Your Log — 78
Key Benefits of Your Activity Log — 79
What's Next for You? Choosing Joy and
Purpose in Your Next Chapter — 82
Summary — 84
Journaling Reflections — 85

Step 5 Stay Connected — 87

Remaining Connected — 87
The Power of Connection — 88
Caring for Old Relationships — 89

What's Next for You? Finding Purpose
Through Giving Back   94
Summary   94
Journaling Reflections   96

Step 6 Remain Mentally and Physically Sharp   98

Staying Mentally and Physically Sharp   98
Staying Sharp: The Key to Thriving in a World of Endless
Possibilities   99
What's Next for You? Embracing Renewal and Growth   100
Practical Activities to Stay Sharp   101
The Benefits of Staying Sharp   102
My Journey to a Sharper Mind   102

Reading has always been my sanctuary. It allows me to
explore new worlds, learn about diverse cultures, and expand
my understanding of the world. Whether it's fiction or
nonfiction, each book I read enriches my mind with new
ideas and perspectives. This habit not only keeps my mind
active but also inspires creativity and curiosity.   103

Writing is another essential part of my routine. It helps me
process my thoughts, reflect on my experiences, and express
myself in a meaningful way. Whether it's journaling, writing
short stories, or even just jotting down notes, this practice
keeps my mind sharp by forcing me to articulate
my thoughts clearly and concisely.   103
Summary   105
Journaling Reflections   106

Step 7 Live a Life of Gratitude   110

The Power of Being Grateful   110
Tapping into Your Gratitude   111
Curious Where to Start Your Gratitude Practice?   112
Summary   114
Journaling Reflections   115

Step 8 Make a Difference—Giving Back — 117

The Importance of Giving Back — 117
The True Meaning of Giving Back — 118
Ways to Give Back — 119
Benefits of Giving Back — 120
What's Next for You? Finding Purpose Beyond the Career You Knew — 122
What's Next for You? Turning Passion into Lasting Impact — 125
What's Next for You? Leading with Purpose Beyond Retirement — 127
Karen Cassidy: Creating a Home for the Forgotten in Their Final Days — 128
What's Next for You? — 131
Living My Life as a Thank You — 131
What's Next for You? — 132
Journaling Reflections — 133

Conclusion — 137
Putting It All Together — 137
Dealing with Loss — 137
Not the End—A New Beginning! — 138
Questions to Ponder — 139
Thought-Provoking Quotes — 142
30-Day Refire Challenge — 144
Appendix Essential Reads to Fuel Your Refire Journey — 144
Programs to Help You Elevate and Embrace Your Refired Life… — 163
The VIP Retreat Day: Your Exclusive Opportunity to Fast-Track Your Next Chapter — 164
Elevate and Ignite: Seminars to Empower Your Refired Journey — 165
Sip & Chat with Cynthia – A Special Gathering for Retired Educators — 166

Dear Teachers:
Your Next Chapter Awaits

Retirement is not the end of your teaching journey—it's the beginning of a new, exciting chapter where you can take all the passion, creativity, and wisdom you've shared in the classroom and channel it into a life that fulfills and inspires you.

After spending more than thirty years in education—starting as an elementary school teacher, transitioning to a guidance counselor, and eventually becoming an assistant high school principal—I've learned the power of reinvention. Each step brought new challenges, new opportunities, and new joys. Now, several years into my retirement journey, I'm inviting you to join me in reimagining what this phase of life can look like.

I know the unique challenges teachers face when they retire—the loss of structure, the sense of purpose that came from shaping young minds, and the camaraderie of the school community. But I also know this: Retirement is brimming with untapped potential.

In Refire— A Roadmap for Teachers to Rediscover Purpose and Joy in Retirement, I'll share my journey and the stories of other educators who have transformed their retirements into times of growth, joy, and meaningful contribution. This book is your guide to rediscovering your purpose, reigniting your passions, and creating a life that excites and fulfills you.

You've spent your career inspiring others—now it's time to inspire yourself. Let Refire show you how to embrace this next chapter with the same curiosity, courage, and creativity you brought to your teaching career. Together, we'll turn retirement into a time of flourishing, connection, and endless possibilities.

Your next chapter is waiting—let's make it extraordinary.

—Cynthia Barnett

Introduction: Is This the Right Book for You?

Are you a teacher nearing retirement or already stepping into this new phase of life? Refire: A Roadmap for Teachers to Rediscover Purpose and Joy in Retirement is designed specifically for educators like you who are ready to embrace the next chapter with purpose and passion. Below are some questions to help you decide if this book is the perfect fit for your journey:

- Have you spent twenty-five, thirty, or more years shaping young minds and now wonder how to channel that same energy into your own life?
- Are you fifty-plus and ready to explore what's next beyond the classroom?
- Do you feel a mix of excitement and apprehension about leaving the structure and community of your teaching career?
- Are you looking for ways to rediscover your purpose and reignite your passions?
- Do you want to design a retirement that incorporates the things you've always dreamed of doing but never had time for?
- Are you seeking clarity on how to spend your time meaningfully and stay connected to others?
- Do you find yourself asking questions like, "What will keep me motivated?" or "How can I continue making a difference?"
- Are you ready to create a life that values experiences, relationships, and personal growth over material possessions?

If you answered "yes" to any of these questions, this book is for you. As a teacher, you've spent your career inspiring others—now it's time to inspire yourself.

By planning ahead and embracing the strategies in Refire, you'll not only ease the transition into retirement but also create a life that excites and fulfills you. Together, we'll explore how to shift gears, find your purpose, and thrive in this new chapter.

Are you ready to refire your life? Let's get started!

The sooner you begin preparing for your next chapter, the better it will be. Investigating your options and creating a focused plan that suits your personality and needs enables you to make significant changes in the way you lead your life and how you feel about the future.

As we embark on this new journey, you may feel a certain sense of anxiety. That is perfectly natural. But it is also why planning ahead is essential. By embracing the strategies I outline in this book, you will cultivate a deep sense of well-being and security, empowering you to thrive in your next chapter.

Finally, by planning early, you will allow yourself the time to try the things you want to do most. You will also give yourself leeway to change your plans or, if necessary, shift your goals.

Marching Toward My Next Chapter: The Birth of Refire

The air was electric with excitement as my students buzzed around me, adjusting their caps and gowns, their laughter and chatter filling the space with energy. The moment had arrived—they were about to march down to the field for their graduation ceremony. But what they didn't know was that I, too, was graduating. My heart raced with anticipation, not just for them, but for myself. It felt as though the universe had aligned, and this wasn't just their moment—it was mine as well. The clouds seemed to part, and the sun broke through, casting a golden glow over the field, as if to welcome me to my next chapter. This wasn't an ending; it was the beginning of something extraordinary. I wasn't retiring—I was refiring.

Helping others reach their next level has always been my

passion, but I've also discovered the transformative power of pursuing adventures that spark your curiosity and excitement. As a lifelong learner and strategic planner, I've spent my life improving not only my own circumstances but also those of others. Along the way, I explored countless self-help avenues, becoming a self-esteem facilitator trained by Jack Canfield, co-author of Chicken Soup for the Soul. I also became a certified life coach, a facilitator for The 7 Habits of Highly Effective People, and completed Marty Seligman's Authentic Happiness Program.

What I didn't realize at the time was these adventures weren't just professional milestones—they were stepping stones preparing me for my own "What's Next?" Each new pursuit helped me uncover strengths, passions, and perspectives that shaped my next chapter. By following what intrigued me, I not only enriched my own life; I also gained the tools to help others do the same.

The truth is pursuing adventures that excite you—whether they're professional, personal, or purely for fun—can open doors you never imagined. They help you grow, adapt, and discover new possibilities, making your next chapter not just a continuation, but a reinvention. What adventure is calling you right now?

Since retiring, I've witnessed many friends who meticulously planned for their financial futures but overlooked the personal, emotional, and psychological dimensions of retirement. As Nancy Schlossberg, author of Retire Smart, Retire Happy, wisely observed, "The biggest mistake people make is not realizing there's a psychological component to retirement." Without a clear sense of purpose or direction, many of my acquaintances have found themselves feeling frustrated, bored, or even lost—some taking jobs simply to fill the void.

In contrast, my journey of preparing for "What's Next?" has been one of discovery, joy, and fulfillment. By embracing new adventures and redefining my purpose, I've created a life that exceeds my wildest dreams. Today, as a retirement lifestyle specialist, cruise lecturer, author, and entrepreneur, I'm thriving in ways I never imagined.

Now, I want to share these lessons with you. Retirement isn't the end of the road—it's the beginning of an exciting new chapter. It's not about slowing down; it's about refiring your passions, reigniting your purpose, and embracing the journey ahead. Are you ready to refire?

The Refire Mission: Rediscovering Purpose and Joy in Retirement

My mission with this book is to inspire millions of educators—and anyone approaching retirement—to rediscover their purpose, reignite their passions, and embrace a fulfilling, joy-filled next chapter. Refire was born from my desire to help those standing at the threshold of retirement, or already navigating their first or second year, to take charge of their newfound freedom and transform it into the most rewarding time of their lives.

Too often, people enter retirement waiting for life to happen to them, unaware that they hold the power to create a vibrant, meaningful future. While many plan meticulously for the financial side of retirement, they overlook the emotional, mental, and spiritual dimensions of this transition. For some, retirement feels like a breath of fresh air; for others, it can feel like stepping into a void. But it doesn't have to be that way.

I wrote this book to challenge the notion that retirement is simply the end of work. Instead, it's an opportunity to Refire—to recharge, reinvigorate, and reconnect with your deepest passions and purpose. It's a chance to design a life that aligns with your dreams, values, and destiny. Think of it this way: We don't make a salad with just lettuce, so why plan retirement with only money in mind? True fulfillment comes from nurturing every aspect of your being—emotional, mental, spiritual, and physical.

My vision for this book is to leave you inspired and equipped with a clear, actionable plan for your next chapter. By the end, you'll not only know what to do with your time, but you'll feel a renewed sense of excitement, purpose, and joy—perhaps more than you've ever experienced before. It's time to Refire and live the life you've always dreamed of. Are you ready?

Refire Your Life: Embracing the Fullness of Retirement

Retirement isn't the end of the road—it's the beginning of a vibrant, new chapter brimming with possibility. Yet, so many retirees overlook the non-financial aspects of this transition, leaving them feeling adrift despite careful financial planning. In fact, a Cornell University study revealed that 57 percent of retirees wish they had prepared more for the emotional, psychological, and purposeful dimensions of retirement.

Take my friend Nancy, for example. After thirty-five years as an educator, she entered retirement financially secure but without a plan for her newfound freedom. Without a sense of purpose, she filled her days with odd jobs, but her spark was missing. Stories like Nancy's inspired me to dig deeper, to explore why so many capable, intelligent people struggle to find joy and meaning in retirement. What I found was a glaring gap in resources—plenty of advice on managing money, but little guidance on how to truly live after leaving a career.

That's why I coined the term refire. Retirement isn't about slowing down, it's about reigniting your passions, reinventing your purpose, and embracing this phase with energy and excitement. Think of it as writing a brand-new book—a thrilling, abundant story about the life you've always dreamed of.

This is your time to explore, grow, and live with intention. With life expectancy climbing and retirees healthier than ever, you could spend twenty to thirty years in retirement—why not make those years extraordinary? Let's replace fear and dread with anticipation and vigor. Let's refire your life and make this chapter the most fulfilling yet. Are you ready to embrace the fullness of retirement?

Living With Purpose and Joy: A Call to Educators

Passion for life isn't reserved for the young or the lucky—it belongs to all of us. As an educator, you've spent your life inspiring others, shaping futures, and making a difference. Now, as you approach retirement, it's time to turn that same energy inward and rediscover what lights you up. Boredom and lack of ambition aren't just unfulfilling—they're unhealthy. The next twenty to thirty years of your life can be your most vibrant, healthful, and meaningful yet.

Let's address a common misconception: Retirement isn't just about golfing or traveling endlessly. Sure, those activities are fun, but what happens when they lose their shine? When the trips end and you're back home, what will give your days purpose? What will make you excited to wake up each morning? The truth is happiness and fulfillment don't come from endless leisure—they come from living with intention, from connecting to your gifts, and from pursuing what truly matters to you.

The Refire mission is about ensuring your retirement is not just a continuation of life, but a reinvention of it. At fifty-five, sixty-five, or even seventy-five, you are still young enough to dream, to grow, and to create. This is your time to uncover the gifts and talents you may have overlooked during your working years. It's your time to connect those gifts to a deeper sense of purpose and craft a life rich with meaning and joy.

As an educator, you've already mastered the art of inspiring others. Now, let's turn that inspiration inward. Together, we'll explore how to harness your strengths, reignite your passions, and design a retirement that is not just successful, but extraordinary.

Ignite Your Next Chapter: The Refire Blueprint for Educators

This book is more than a roadmap—it's a call to action. It will help you uncover exciting alternatives, set meaningful goals, and design a life that reflects your dreams, not someone else's expectations. Through the strategies in Refire, you'll embark on an inner pilgrimage, reconnecting with the passions and values that make you who you are. It's about moving your dreams from the back burner to the forefront, where they can blaze into a vibrant reality.

Retirement is your time to soar. The years you've spent teaching, mentoring, and navigating life have gifted you with wisdom, resilience, and strength. Now, you have the opportunity to channel those gifts into a life of deeper meaning and joy. Each chapter of Refire is designed to guide you through this transformation:

- Shift Gears: Redefine your identity and embrace personal growth.
- Discover Your Life Purpose: Reignite the passions that bring you joy.
- Discover Your Strengths: Leverage your unique talents to thrive.
- Manage Your Life and Time: Balance leisure with purpose-driven activities.
- Stay Connected: Build meaningful relationships and community ties.
- Remain Sharp Mentally and Physically: Prioritize cognitive and physical health.
- Live a Life of Gratitude: Cultivate thankfulness for a positive outlook.
- Make a Difference: Enrich your life by giving back and mentoring others.

This is your moment to embrace the possibilities ahead. Let Refire inspire you to craft a life of passion, purpose, and joy Most of the stories featured in each chapter come from teachers, supplemented by a few from individuals who have successfully refired their lives.

STEP I
SHIFT GEARS

REDEFINING IDENTITY IN RETIREMENT

"We delight in the beauty of the butterfly, but rarely admit the changes it has gone through to achieve that beauty."

— *Maya Angelou*

This quote emphasizes the beauty in transformation, capturing the essence of shifting gears and embracing a new identity in retirement.

"You must do the thing you think you cannot do."

— *Eleanor Roosevelt*

This quote encourages stepping out of comfort zones, an essential part of redefining oneself in a new chapter of life.

Shift Gears: Redefining Your Purpose as an Educator in Retirement

If you want to embrace the retirement life you've envisioned, the first step is to shift gears. For educators, this is a powerful process of redefining who you are beyond the classroom. It's about transitioning from a career spent inspiring others to a new chapter where you inspire yourself. As Wayne Dyer said, "If you are what you do, then when you don't, you aren't." That's why this shift is so essential—it's your opportunity to move from "What I do" to "Who I am."

As teachers, our identities are often tied to our roles. We wear our titles like badges of honor—"I'm a teacher," "I'm a principal," "I'm a counselor." But now, it's time to disentangle your identity from your job and rediscover the essence of you. This isn't about leaving behind the impact you've made; it's about building on it in new and exciting ways.

Think of it like teaching a student to take their first steps in learning. Each step is uncertain but filled with potential. Or imagine Tarzan swinging through the jungle—he has to let go of one vine to grab the next. That's what this transition is: letting go of the familiar to reach for
something extraordinary.

When people ask me now what I do, I proudly say, "I am a life coach." That label reflects my passions and values, not just my past. You, too, have the power to redefine yourself, to let go of the old vine and reach for the next. This is your moment to step forward, one exciting step at a time, and create a life that truly reflects who you are. Are you ready to shift gears and embrace this incredible new chapter?

Consequences of Not Shifting Gears

As an educator, your career has been more than a job—it's been a calling, a purpose, and a source of pride. But when retirement comes, clinging to the identity of "teacher" without redefining who you are beyond the classroom can have serious consequences. Shifting gears isn't just a suggestion, it's a necessity for a fulfilling and joyful next chapter.

For some, the idea of change feels overwhelming. It's tempting to hold on tightly to what's familiar, to keep things as they've always been. But resisting this shift can leave you feeling stuck, unable to move forward, and disconnected from the vibrant possibilities of life after teaching. Without the structure and identity that your career provided, a sense of loss can creep in, and for many, this can lead to feelings of depression or aimlessness.

The key to avoiding this is to embrace the process of reevaluating your identity outside the parameters of your profession. This isn't about leaving behind the impact you've made as a teacher—it's about building on it. It's about taking that same passion, wisdom, and creativity you poured into your students and channeling it into new pursuits that align with your values and dreams.

For many educators, this will be the first time they've taken such a deep look inward. But this work is trans-formative. By shifting gears, you'll discover who you are beyond the classroom and open the door to a retirement filled with purpose, joy, and growth. Are you ready to embrace this new journey?

From Administrator to Actress: Janice's Journey to Rediscovering Herself After Retirement

Janice was a self-admitted workaholic. She completely over-identified with being an administrator. She became depressed and fearful when faced with the decision of what to do after she retired. Because she identified so completely with her role and function as an administrator, she feared becoming worthless and incapable of contributing to the world as she had before.

As an administrator, Janice had a lot of authority and was constantly busy, so she had little time to think of anything else but running a building. Plus, people were constantly coming to her to solve their problems. She carried a heavy load, a lot of people were accountable to her, and when she finally left, it was like she was stripped of everything.

Retirement was such a shock to Janice's system that sometimes she went back to the school just to say hello. But, of course, after a while, that began to wear off. So, in working with her, I had to help her come to grips with who she really was. We looked for ways she could transfer some of those same skills to other life options and bring the good parts of her job into her new life. She needed to still enjoy the feeling of being needed and having meaning in her life.

Because Janice used to really enjoy the theater, she started going to some theater productions. She ended up taking a small part in a production. That made her feel very needed, especially when the audience gave her a standing ovation. That experience helped to satisfy her need to be in the spotlight. It gave her a new lease on life, and it helped her shift gears.

Rediscovering Your Values: A Guide for Educators to Thrive in Retirement

As educators, your career has been a reflection of your core values—whether it was fostering curiosity, nurturing potential, or inspiring growth. These values didn't disappear when you left the classroom; they're still within you, ready to be expressed in new and exciting ways. Shifting gears into retirement is about recognizing those values and proactively creating a life that aligns with them.

The word "retirement" can feel limiting, even unhealthy—it carries the word "tire," after all! But this next chapter isn't about slowing down; it's about refiring. Start early, before you leave your job, to ease the transition. Take time to reflect on what truly matters to you. What hobbies or passions did you set aside while dedicating yourself to your students? Were you once a painter, a gardener, or a writer? Now is the time to revisit those dreams and reframe them in the context of what you want to accomplish in the next twenty to thirty years.

Stephen Covey's advice to "begin with the end in mind" is a powerful tool here. Picture yourself at eighty-five, surrounded by loved ones celebrating your life. What do you want them to say about you? What legacy—beyond the classroom—do you want to leave behind? This isn't about financial or measurable success; it's about the human impact you'll have.

To redefine yourself, start by asking reflective questions: Who was the person behind the teacher? What traits—creativity, resourcefulness, compassion—defined you? Then, turn to those who know you best. Ask them to share your strengths and life's defining moments. You'll begin to see a vibrant picture of who you are beyond your job title.

This process isn't just about rediscovery—it's about reigniting your passion and creating a life filled with purpose, joy, and meaning.

Taking Inventory of Your Talents

This is a time to take inventory of what you're best at, turning your focus away from your perceived weaknesses so you can put that focus into discovering and strengthening your skills, aptitudes, and talents.

In some cases—for example, educators and trainers who've worked in corporate environments—you might not have had the opportunity to really express your creative side. What you're taking stock of may be partially or entirely hidden from you and can only come to the surface when you begin to make inventories of your behaviors.

Were you an organizer and a leader at work? Or did you sit quietly and daydream of ways to make the process better, even if you knew you couldn't express it? You will be very surprised at what you find out when you begin, with pen in hand and paper before you, to list your traits, behavior patterns, strong points, and major turning points.

In the process of redefinition and through this process of self-inquiry and shaping, it is important to come up with a new title. Now, instead of a marketing director, you are, say, an adventurer, the hero or heroine in your own epic story of life. Or you are an experiencer of life, a pursuer of truth, a laid-back connoisseur of new experiences.

As a matter of fact, I interviewed a couple recently who retired pretty early and who call themselves adventurers. Tired of the rat race, they decided they wanted to retire early. They both had very strenuous and stressful jobs. They were only seeing each other passing in the night, and they decided that was not a meaningful way for them to live and be connected with each other.

So, they both pre-planned and saved all the money they could. They decided to travel, and now they may live for five months in Thailand or a year in Mexico, or six weeks in the Hawaiian Islands. They have traveled and lived almost all over the world. So, their self-proclaimed title is—adventurers.

Shifting Gears: How Akaish and Billy Transformed Retirement into a Life of Adventure and Purpose

Akaish and Billy's journey is not just a story of early retirement; it's a tale of transformation, adventure, and lifelong learning. Married more than four decades ago in the charming coastal town of Santa Cruz, California, they first crossed paths in an environment steeped in culinary delight and entrepreneurial spirit. Billy, a French-trained chef, had honed his skills in prestigious restaurants, while Akaish managed the operations, ensuring their restaurant, Luther's, became a local sensation.

Despite their success, the daily grind began to wear on them, and they yearned for more than the restaurant could offer. In 1989, after a decade of serving the Santa Cruz community, they evaluated their lives and aspirations. Realizing they had the means to shift gears, they decided it was time for a radical change.

On January 14, 1991, at the young age of thirty-eight, Akaish and Billy retired from their careers to embark on what Billy affectionately calls their "perpetual gypsy schedule." They sold their home and most possessions, taking their first steps toward a nomadic life with a move to Nevis, a tiny island in the West Indies. This bold move marked the beginning of their adventures across the globe, from the vibrant landscapes of the West Indies and Venezuela to the bustling streets of Canada and the cultural richness of Central and Southeast Asia.

Their early days of retirement were filled with discovery and spontaneity. They traveled without reservations, often arriving in new cities and finding accommodations on the fly, guided by nothing but Lonely Planet and Rough Guides. Over the years, as technology evolved, so did their travel style. Today, they plan their journeys with online tools and enjoy the comforts of upscale hotels, first-class transportation, and extended stays that offer a deeper connection to the places they visit.

Beyond just traveling, Akaish and Billy have dedicated significant portions of their journey to volunteer work, contributing to communities in meaningful ways. Whether teaching English in Mexico, constructing tennis courts in Chapala, or importing an electronic scoreboard for a local gymnasium, their retirement is defined by service and positive impact.

Reflecting on their lives, Akaish and Billy recognize the unconventional path they've taken—a path not driven by wealth but by the richness of experience and the joy of sharing with others. Their story is a testament to the power of redefining one's identity after retirement and embracing life's second acts with enthusiasm and purpose.

As they continue to explore new destinations and cultures, Akaish and Billy's lives are a profound reminder that retirement can be the beginning of the most vibrant chapters of our lives, filled with adventures, new lessons, and the freedom to live on one's own terms. Their story is not just inspiring—it's a call to rethink what's possible in our later years.

What's Next for You? Shifting Gears to a Life of Purpose and Adventure

Akaish and Billy's story is proof that retirement isn't about slowing down—it's about shifting gears into a life of greater freedom, adventure, and fulfillment. They dared to step away from the traditional path, redefining what retirement could look like by embracing travel, service, and lifelong discovery.

Now, it's your turn.

✶ What dreams have you put on hold, waiting for the "right time"?

✶ How can you shift gears and create a retirement that excites and inspires you?

✶ What small step can you take today to move toward a more fulfilling future?

Like Akaish and Billy, you have the power to design your next chapter on your own terms—whether that means exploring new places, giving back, or simply stepping into a lifestyle that aligns with your deepest passions.

→ **Your next adventure starts now. Where will it take you?**

Mickey Revenaugh: From Edtech Pioneer to Transformative Author

Mickey Revenaugh's journey from an educational technology (edtech) innovator to author intertwines her deep-seated passion for education with her roots, crafting a narrative that's both inspiring and trans-formative. Mickey, originally a pioneering figure behind the launch of the federal E-rate program and Connections Academy, has long been a champion for democratizing education through technology. Her work has not only paved new paths for online K-12 education, but it has laid the groundwork for equitable access across diverse learning communities.

As she transitioned into retirement, Mickey channeled her extensive experience into writing a book that captures the evolving landscape of non-traditional education. Her memoir, How Mickey Revenaugh Says We Can Deliver on the Promise of Online Education, is more than just a recount of her professional achievements—it's a deep dive into the lessons learned throughout her career and the potential of online learning to level the educational playing field.

Throughout the COVID-19 pandemic, Mickey observed the rapid shift to remote schooling and recognized the necessity to share her insights on creating robust online education systems. Her book critiques the hurried patchwork of virtual learning solutions implemented during the pandemic, contrasting them with the thoughtfully designed program at Connections Academy, which integrates synchronous and asynchronous learning to empower students.

Mickey argues for the improvement of online programs beyond emergency solutions, advocating for a holistic approach that addresses the digital divide, enhances teacher training, and fosters genuine engagement among students. Her book not only reflects on her experiences but acts as a guide for educators and policymakers aiming to harness the full potential of online education.

In her writings, Mickey leverages her background to propose three trans-formative educational policies: integrating K-12 education into a broader system of lifelong learning, ensuring universal high-speed internet access, and providing extensive professional development for educators. She envisions a future where every learner has the tools and opportunities to succeed, influenced by her professional journey and personal commitment to educational equity.

Mickey's narrative is enriched with personal anecdotes, including the poignant moment following the 9/11 attacks that inspired the name "Connections Academy." Her story is a compelling testament to how one's career expertise can illuminate retirement, turning it into a phase of purpose-driven authorship and continued advocacy for change.

Through her book and ongoing engagements, Mickey Revenaugh remains a vital voice in education, inspiring a new generation to think creatively about how we teach and learn in an increasingly digital world. Her work demonstrates how retiring from a career doesn't mean stepping back from making a difference; rather, it opens new avenues for sharing wisdom and inspiring future transformations.

What's Next for You? Shifting Gears from Career to Purpose-Driven Impact

Mickey Revenaugh's story is a powerful reminder that retirement isn't the end of making a difference—it's an opportunity to shift gears and apply your life's work in new, meaningful ways. She transformed decades of experience in educational technology and policy into a mission to shape the future of online learning, proving that your expertise doesn't expire when your career does.

Now, it's your turn.

★ How can you take your professional experience and turn it into something that inspires and informs others?

- What impact do you still want to make in your field, community, or the world?
- What passions have been waiting for you to have the time and freedom to pursue them?

Like Mickey, your next chapter can be filled with purpose, influence, and creativity—whether it's writing, mentoring, advocating for change, or building something entirely new.

→ Your legacy is still being written. What will you create next?

Joe Sirico: From Master Plumber to Inspiring Educator

After a successful career spanning decades as a plumber, Joe Sirico traded in his wrenches for textbooks and lesson plans. Motivated by a desire to pass on his extensive knowledge and ignite a passion for plumbing in future generations, Joe embarked on a new journey as a classroom teacher.

Joe's transition wasn't immediate; it required him to return to school to earn the necessary certifications to teach. Embracing this challenge head-on, he took the plunge with enthusiasm, determined to make a significant difference. Now, five years into his teaching career, Joe has become an influential figure in the plumbing and heating program at a vocational school.

In his classroom, Joe combines practical skills with academic theory, instructing students in construction safety, measuring, blueprint reading, and the calculations necessary for plumbing and heating systems. His lessons cover the essentials—drainage fixture units, water supply fixture units, gas pipe sizing, and hydronic heating applications. But Joe's teaching goes beyond the technical; he instills in his students the importance of energy efficiency, renewable energy, and conservation practices, preparing them for the future of the industry.

Through Joe's program, students not only gain up to 720 hours of instruction toward their P-2 apprenticeship, but they may also receive up to 1,500 hours toward a career-affiliated apprenticeship upon graduation and employer acceptance. This opportunity opens numerous doors for young tradespeople entering a field that is both lucrative and in high demand.

Joe's commitment to his students and his craft reflects his profound belief in the opportunities that a career in plumbing presents. By sharing his expertise and passion, Joe Sirico not only enriches the lives of his students but ensures the vital trade of plumbing continues to evolve and adapt in an ever-changing world.

Beyond the workshop and classroom, Joe also serves as the coach for the girls' volleyball team, bringing the same passion and dedication to the court that he does to his shop. His dual role as a teacher and coach enriches the student experience, fostering both teamwork and individual skill development.

His story is a testament to the power of change and the positive impact one individual can have on the lives of many, proving it's never too late to pursue a new path and make a difference.

Joe Sirico's journey proves that it's never too late to pivot, learn, and make a lasting impact. After decades as a successful plumber, he shifted gears to become a teacher, ensuring that future generations are equipped with the skills, knowledge, and passion to thrive in a critical trade. His story is a reminder that retirement or career transition isn't about slowing down—it's about finding new ways to contribute and inspire.

Now, it's your turn.

✶ What skills or expertise do you have that could benefit others?

- How can you turn your passion into mentor ship, education, or leadership?
- What bold step could you take today to start a fulfilling new chapter?

Like Joe, your experiences are valuable, and there's always an opportunity to pass them on, whether through teaching, coaching, mentoring, or leading in your community.

→ Your next great contribution is waiting. How will you make an impact?

Navigating Dreams: Eugenia Chinsman's Second Act as a Global Travel Architect

After a fulfilling career in corporate environments, Eugenia Chinsman discovered a new passion that transformed her retirement into an adventure of its own. As a highly skilled travel advisor with eighteen years of experience, Eugenia specializes in crafting unforgettable travel experiences, from African safaris to destination weddings and cultural tours in West Africa.

Eugenia's journey into the world of travel was not a sudden leap but a gradual transition fueled by her lifelong passion for exploring diverse cultures and destinations. This passion was deeply influenced by her husband's career with the United Nations, which allowed them to travel extensively. Witnessing the richness of different cultures first-hand inspired Eugenia to share these experiences with others, which ultimately led her to become a travel agent.

The decision to change her career path came from a desire to have more time to explore her interests and share her extensive knowledge of global cultures with potential travelers. This move allowed her to blend her personal interests with a professional pursuit, making her work deeply fulfilling.

Eugenia's story is not just about changing careers; it's about transforming her entire life's direction based on her core passions. She embodies the spirit of reinvention, proving that it's never too late to pursue what truly makes one happy. Through her travel agency, she continues to inspire and enable others to explore the world, emphasizing the importance of experiencing new cultures and traditions. Her approach is not just about visiting places but truly connecting with them, which she facilitates with a deep understanding and respect for the destinations she promotes.

This transition from a corporate role to a travel expert highlights the power of following one's passions into retirement, turning what could be the end of a professional journey into the beginning of a much more personal and rewarding one. Eugenia Chinsman's story is a testament to the joys and fulfillment that come from embracing change and pursuing what truly ignites one's spirit.

What's Next for You? Turning Passion into Purpose

Eugenia Chinsman's story proves that retirement isn't an end—it's an opportunity to shift gears and create a life filled with passion and purpose. She seamlessly transitioned from a corporate career to becoming a highly sought-after travel advisor, blending her love for exploration with her expertise to help others experience the world in meaningful ways.

Now, it's your turn.

* What passions have been calling to you that you've put on hold?
* How can you turn your life experiences into something fulfilling and impactful?
* What small step can you take today to start a new adventure in your next chapter?

Like Eugenia, you have the power to transform your interests into a rewarding and exciting second act—whether that means exploring a new career, launching a passion project, or embracing a completely different path.

→ **Your journey is just beginning. Where will it take you next?**

Summary

This chapter delved into the transformative journey educators must take as they transition from defining themselves by their professional roles to embracing a more personal and fulfilling identity. Retirement is not an end, but a beginning—a chance to rediscover who you are beyond the classroom and realign with the core values that have always guided you. For teachers, this shift means letting go of the work-centered self and stepping into a new purpose, one that reflects your passions, dreams, and the legacy you want to create in this exciting next chapter of life.

Key Takeaways:

- Redefining yourself in retirement involves transitioning from "what I do" to "who I am."
- Align your new identity with your core values for a more fulfilling retirement.
- Embrace the opportunities retirement provides to rediscover hobbies, passions, and talents that were sidelined during your working life.

Journaling Reflections

As you embark on this transformative journey of self-discovery, reflection, and growth, the act of journaling will become one of your most powerful tools. Through journaling, you will bring clarity to your thoughts, connect more deeply with your heart's desires, and uncover the wisdom within you that will help guide your next chapter.

Before you begin, find a quiet, peaceful space where you can reflect without distraction. This is your time—your personal retreat. You may want to put on your favorite calming music, light a candle, or surround yourself with items that bring you joy and relaxation.

Consider treating yourself to a beautiful journal, a space dedicated to capturing your reflections, dreams, and intentions. Whether it's an ornate notebook that inspires you or a simple one that gets the job done, let it be a place where your thoughts come alive on the page. If you prefer, typing your thoughts digitally works just as well—the key is to create a space where you can honestly and openly explore.

Now, as you delve into the journaling questions ahead, take your time. Allow your thoughts to flow freely. There is no right or wrong answer—this is a process of reflection and discovery, and every insight is valuable. Your journal will be your companion as you re-imagine, refire, and elevate your life to new heights.

Take a deep breath, open your heart, and let your pen—or keyboard—be the guide to uncovering the next chapter of your extraordinary journey.

How has your professional identity shaped how you see yourself? What aspects of your identity do you want to carry into retirement, and what new elements would you like to explore?

_____
_____
_____

1. What fears or challenges arise when you think about letting go of your old roles? How can you re-frame these fears as opportunities for growth?

_____
_____
_____

2. What interests, hobbies, or passions have you set aside in the past? How can you make space for them in this new chapter of life?

_____
_____
_____

3. If you could describe your ideal life beyond work, what would it look like? How can you begin taking steps toward that vision today?

_____
_____
_____

4. What is one habit or mindset from your working life that no longer serves you? How can you begin to shift away from it?

_____
_____
_____

STEP 2
FIND YOUR PURPOSE

DISCOVERING YOUR PURPOSE

"The two most important days in your life are the day you are born and the day you find out why." — *Author Unknown*

This quote highlights the importance of discovering your deeper purpose, especially in retirement when you're free to pursue what truly fulfills you.

"Your purpose in life is to find your purpose and give your whole heart and soul to it." — *Buddha*

This quote encourages full-hearted commitment to living with purpose in the next chapter of life.

Redefining Purpose: A New Chapter for Educators

This chapter explores the profound and transformative journey educators face as they transition from defining themselves by their professional roles to embracing a deeply personal and fulfilling identity. For teachers, retirement is not the end of a meaningful life—it's the beginning of a new chapter, one filled with opportunities to rediscover who you are beyond the classroom walls. It's a chance to realign with the core values that have always guided your work, but now in ways that reflect your passions, dreams, and the legacy you want to leave behind.

For educators, this shift requires letting go of the work-centered self—a self that has been so deeply tied to the mission of teaching and nurturing others—and stepping into a new purpose. This purpose is as unique as each individual. Just as every student you taught had their own story, your next chapter will be shaped by your own. Whether it's reigniting a love for art, mentoring in your community, or pursuing a long-forgotten dream, this is your time to create a life that reflects the values and passions that have always driven you.

Purpose takes many forms. I've seen people dedicate themselves to causes as diverse as caring for children with disabilities, writing books, or traveling the world to share their wisdom. Each purpose is as unique as the person living it. For teachers, the legacy you create in this next chapter will be just as impactful as the one you built in the classroom—perhaps even more so. This is your moment to embrace the freedom to define yourself anew and live a life that inspires not only others but also yourself.

Work With Purpose: A Guide for Educators in Retirement

For educators, the transition into retirement often brings a longing for structure and purpose—two things that teaching naturally provides. It's no surprise that many retired teachers find themselves returning to work in some capacity, not out of necessity, but to fill their days with meaning and avoid the stagnation that can come with too much free time. After all, as a teacher, you've spent your career making an impact, and that drive doesn't simply disappear.

If you do decide to reenter the workforce, the key is to align your new role with your values and passions. This isn't about just filling time or creating structure, it's about finding work that feels like an extension of who you are. For example, many retired educators thrive in roles that allow them to continue inspiring others, such as tutoring, mentoring, or working in educational nonprofits. Others may explore entirely new fields that reflect their personal interests, like volunteering at a library, working in a museum, or even starting a small business.

The beauty of this stage in life is that you have the freedom to choose work that truly resonates with you. Whether it's part-time, volunteer-based, or entrepreneurial, the work you pursue should be an expression of your core values and purpose. Think of it as an opportunity to channel your creativity, wisdom, and experience into something that brings you joy and fulfillment. What kind of work would feel meaningful to you in this next chapter?

Determining Your Goals: A Guide for Educators in Retirement

As teachers, you've spent your career inspiring others, solving problems, and meeting challenges head-on. Retirement is your opportunity to channel that same energy into goals that bring you joy, purpose, and fulfillment. When setting your retirement goals, consider these four essential criteria:

1. Do something you truly love. What activities or passions have you set aside during your teaching years?
2. Pursue a goal you feel deeply connected to. Whether it's

mentoring, volunteering, or exploring a creative pursuit, choose something that excites you.
3. Contribute something valuable to your own life. This is your time to grow, learn, and thrive.
4. Contribute to others' lives. Your experience as an educator gives you a unique ability to make a difference in your community or beyond.

These steps require effort—just as you encouraged your students to dig deep, you'll need to do the same. Start by listing the things you love and exploring how they connect to your purpose. If you decide to take on a job or volunteer role, let it align with your passions and values. That way, your work becomes meaningful and fulfilling.

The Value of Challenges

As educators, you know the power of a good challenge—it's what keeps your classroom dynamic and engaging. In retirement, challenges remain just as important. They give you a sense of purpose, stretch your abilities, and bring the satisfaction of accomplishment. Whether it's learning a new skill, tackling a creative project, or solving problems in your community, embracing challenges will keep you energized and fulfilled.

What passions or challenges are calling to you as you step into this exciting new chapter?

Transitioning into a Purposeful Life

As a teacher, retirement is a profound rite of passage—a moment to celebrate the incredible impact you've made and to embrace the exciting opportunities ahead. Think of this transition not as an end, but as the beginning of a new chapter. Why not mark it with a celebration? Hosting a "refiring" party, rather than a retirement party, reframes this

milestone as the start of a grand new adventure.
When people ask, "Are you retiring?" you can proudly say, "No, I'm refiring!"

This celebration is your bon voyage party, sending you off on a journey toward a new purpose. As educators, you've spent years inspiring others to dream big—now it's your turn. Without the constraints of a rigid schedule, you have the freedom to pursue your passions and explore what truly lights you up.

Ask yourself: What do you love to do? Beyond teaching, what activities bring you joy and fulfillment? Perhaps you've always loved mentoring, creating, or mediating. Maybe you've dreamed of writing a book, volunteering in your community, or even starting a new venture. This is your time to dream boldly and align your next steps with your passions and strengths.

For example, if you've always loved decorating, like I do, you might channel that creativity into designing spaces for others or even teaching workshops. The key is to connect your hobbies and interests to a larger purpose—one that reflects your values and the legacy you want to build.

What dreams have been waiting for you to refire them? This is your moment to embrace them fully and step into this next chapter with excitement and purpose.

What gives you the most joy in life? Who would you love to be and why? What gives you the greatest sense of meaning? And what do you feel is your true service obligation in life? When you have written down the answers to those questions, review those answers and circle the one that speaks the most to you—the one that gives you a deep sense of purpose.

Finding Purpose Beyond Retirement: How I Refired My Life Through Amazing Girls Science

Retirement is often seen as a time to slow down, but for

me, it became the launchpad for one of the most rewarding chapters of my life. During this period, I discovered a new purpose that not only reignited my passion but allowed me to positively and significantly impact others. Here is how I founded Amazing Girls Science, a nonprofit organization dedicated to empowering young girls through science, technology, engineering, art, and mathematics (STEAM).

The journey began when I stumbled upon a startling statistic in a research study by the American Association of University Women titled "Why So Few? Women in Science, Technology, Engineering, and Mathematics." It highlighted a significant gender gap in the STEAM fields that hadn't crossed my mind during my career years. Despite women making up half of the US workforce, they held only 25 percent of the jobs in technical or computing fields. Furthermore, while the number of tech jobs was increasing, the amount of tech talent, especially female, was not keeping pace. This disparity wasn't just a gap; it was a gaping chasm waiting to be addressed.

Compelled by these findings, I felt a powerful drive to do something that would make a difference. Retirement had given me free time, but more importantly, it provided me the freedom to use that time to fuel my passion for change and empowerment.

With the vision clear in my mind, I launched Amazing Girls Science. The goal was simple yet ambitious: To ignite girls' interest in STEAM and help them become the innovative and creative thinkers needed to meet twenty-first-century challenges. The program was designed to encourage not only academic engagement in STEAM but to foster core life skills such as self-confidence, self-esteem, curiosity, problem-solving, and positive risk-taking.

The impact was immediate and profound. Girls who never saw themselves as scientists or engineers were suddenly envisioning careers in those fields. They were solving complex problems, designing projects, and most importantly, they were dreaming big. Their enthusiasm was contagious, and the community took notice. Amazing Girls Science was featured in the CBS Martin Luther King Fulfilling the Dream TV program, which focused on individuals in the community who give back.

The recognition didn't stop there. I was honored by the Connecticut Technology Council with its Community Innovation & Leadership Award. Even more humbling was winning the Inaugural AARP Purpose Prize, which recognized the substantial contributions of Amazing Girls Science in igniting the spark in girls for STEAM.

This venture transformed my retirement into a dynamic and purposeful mission. It wasn't just about filling my days but filling them in such a way that I could give back and create lasting change. Each workshop, each smile on the girls' faces, each moment of discovery reminded me that retirement was my chance to do something powerful to change lives.

Today, Amazing Girls Science continues to grow, each program building on the last to inspire more girls to explore STEAM. The need for gender parity in these fields is as critical as ever, and I am committed to championing this cause. It's a testament to how retirement can be a beginning, not an end, and a reminder that we're never too old to dream a new dream or ignite a new passion.

In reflecting on this journey, I realize that Amazing Girls Science did more than just fill a gap in STEAM education; it filled a space in my heart that yearned for purpose beyond professional achievement. It is a beacon that lights up not just my life but the lives of countless young girls who now believe they, too, can contribute to and excel in the world of science and technology.

Capturing New Horizons: Tom Kretsch's Inspiring Journey from Teacher to Celebrated Photographer

Tom Kretsch's inspiring journey from physical education

teacher to accomplished photographer beautifully illustrates that retirement is not an ending, but a gateway to new beginnings and expanded horizons. After dedicating thirty-six years to shaping young minds through physical education, Tom embraced a long-held interest in photography, transforming it from a hobby into a full-fledged artistic pursuit. His story serves as a powerful reminder that our later years can be the most creative, fulfilling, and joyful phase of our lives.

Upon retiring, Tom didn't settle into a quiet life. Instead, he launched "Peaceful Places," a venture that became the vehicle through which he could express his vision and invite others to find serenity in the world around them. This bold step into a new career demonstrates how retirement can be an opportunity to explore passions that may have simmered beneath the surface for years, waiting for the right moment to flourish.

Tom's photographic style, distinguished by its focus on light, texture, form, and color, transcends mere documentation. His work transforms ordinary scenes into havens of tranquility, inviting viewers to pause and find peace in the midst of life's chaos. Drawing inspiration from the artistic legacies of the Wyeth family and Edward Hopper, Kretsch developed a unique approach that blends realism with a painterly quality, showcasing how retirement can be a time of continued learning and artistic growth.

While Tom's artistic journey began in his hometown of Westport, Connecticut, it quickly expanded to encompass diverse landscapes from the rustic charm of Tuscany to the vibrant scenes of Mexico. This global exploration highlights how retirement can open doors to new adventures and experiences, broadening one's perspective and enriching life in unexpected ways.

Tom's dedication to his craft has not gone unnoticed, with his work garnering numerous awards and featured in fine arts festivals throughout New England. This recognition serves as a powerful affirmation of his decision to pursue photography and the quality of his artistic vision, demonstrating that success and recognition can come at any stage of life.

Despite his success, Tom remains deeply connected to his community, actively participating in local arts centers and undertaking significant projects such as the office corridor installation in Westport. These endeavors show how retirement can be a time to give back to one's community, sharing the wisdom and talents acquired over a lifetime.

Tom's book, On the Road—Five Visions, stands as a testament to his artistic journey, exploring the themes and inspirations that have shaped his photographic career. This publication not only showcases his work but serves as an inspiration for others contemplating new ventures in their retirement years.

Tom's story is a beacon of hope and inspiration for anyone approaching or already in retirement. It reminds us that our later years can be filled with creativity, purpose, and joy. By following his heart and dedicating himself to mastering a new craft, Tom exemplifies how retirement can be a springboard to new adventures, continued learning, and meaningful contributions to society.

His journey encourages others to embrace new passions, pursue lifelong learning, and find ways to contribute to their communities through their talents. It proves that retirement is not about slowing down, but about seizing the opportunity to live life to its fullest, exploring new horizons, and finding fulfillment in unexpected places. Tom's story is a powerful reminder that it's never too late to pursue your dreams and that the golden years can truly be a time of golden opportunities.

What's Next for You?

Tom Kretsch's journey proves that retirement isn't about slowing down—it's about shifting gears and embracing new passions. After thirty-six years as a physical education teacher, he transformed a lifelong interest in photography into a fulfilling second career, proving that the next phase of life can be just as dynamic, creative, and rewarding as the first.

Now, it's your turn.

- ✷ What passion or interest has been waiting for you to have the time and space to pursue it?

- ✷ How can you take a small step today toward a new creative
or professional pursuit?

- ✷ What legacy do you want to build in this next stage of your life?

Like Tom Kretsch, you have the opportunity to redefine what your next chapter looks like—whether that means exploring a new hobby, starting a business, giving back to your community, or traveling the world.

→ **Your greatest adventure may still be ahead. Where will it take you?**

Transforming Passion into Purpose: Janet Evelyn's Inspiring Journey

Janet Evelyn's journey from a seasoned entrepreneur to the founder of the Norwalk International Cultural Exchange is a story of passion transformed into purpose. After three decades as a marketing and advertising professional, Janet felt a calling that extended beyond the corporate sphere.

Her career had equipped her with invaluable skills in branding and project management, but it was her innate entrepreneurial spirit that drove her toward a more culturally enriching venture.

The transition wasn't just a career change; it was a life transformation. Janet's deep-seated appreciation for the arts and culture, honed through years of planning entertainment and promotional events, naturally guided her toward the creation of a platform that could celebrate and educate others about global cultures. This seed grew into the Norwalk International Cultural Exchange (NICE).

This organization was born out of Janet's vision to foster understanding and appreciation of diverse cultures. By leveraging her background in marketing, Janet could strategically promote cultural awareness and inclusivity. The Exchange didn't just host events; it became a cultural hub that offered a window to the world, right in the heart of Fairfield County.

Janet's commitment to her new path was steadfast. She recognized that to truly make a difference, you must harness your skills and channel them toward your passions. Her advice to anyone in the second half of their life is clear: Find what ignites your passion and pursue it with all the creativity and innovation you possess. For Janet, that meant turning her professional expertise into a tool for cultural education and enrichment.

Under Janet's leadership, the Norwalk International Cultural Exchange flourished, bringing diverse cultural programming to the community and becoming a pivotal force in cultural education. Janet's story is not just about changing careers; it's about using one's life experiences to give back and enhance the lives of others.

NICE's educational initiatives are rooted in folk and traditional art forms, expanding beyond their annual NICE Festival to provide year-round cultural enrichment. The programs are specifically tailored to promote understanding and appreciation of diverse global heritages among students.

By bringing global experiences to life in local schools, NICE's educational programs are playing a crucial role in promoting cultural understanding and diversity among Norwalk's youth.

Janet's journey illustrates that it's never too late to reshape your path and impact the world positively. Her story encourages all of us to explore, engage, and contribute, reminding us that our next chapter could be the most rewarding yet.

What's Next for You? Turning Experience into Impact

Janet Evelyn's story is a powerful testament to the idea that it's never too late to channel your passion into something meaningful. She leveraged decades of experience in marketing and entrepreneurship to create the Norwalk International Cultural Exchange (NICE)—a platform that fosters cultural awareness, inclusivity, and education. Her journey proves that the next phase of life can be about giving back, inspiring others, and creating lasting impact.

Now, it's your turn.

✴ What passion or cause has been calling to you?
✴ How can you use your experience and skills to make a difference in your community?
✴ What small step can you take today to move toward a purpose-driven second act?

Like Janet, you have the power to redefine what your next chapter looks like—whether through entrepreneurship, community service, cultural advocacy, or creative expression.

→ **Your greatest impact may still be ahead. Where will it take you?**

Janet Stewart's Inspiring Journey of Reinvention in Retirement: From Kitchen to Keyboard

Janet Stewart's transition from a Culinary Arts and Hospitality instructor to an accomplished author is a captivating tale of self-discovery and personal growth that exemplifies the transformative potential of retirement. Her story serves as an inspiring beacon for those entering their golden years, demonstrating that life's later chapters can be filled with unexpected adventures and newfound passions.

Born in the verdant island of St. Vincent, Janet's culinary journey began in her grandmother's kitchen. The rich tapestry of flavors and techniques passed down through generations ignited a lifelong passion for cooking and storytelling. These early experiences would shape her future career and ultimately influence her writing.

Janet's love for food and hospitality led her to a fulfilling career as a Culinary Arts and Hospitality instructor. For years, she imparted her knowledge and passion to countless students, nurturing the next generation of culinary professionals. Her classroom became a stage where she could combine her love for cooking with her natural flair for storytelling.

As retirement approached, Janet found herself at a familiar crossroads. The prospect of endless free time was both exciting and daunting. While she briefly considered continuing her teaching career at a community college, fate had different plans for her.

The desire to connect with her grandchildren and leave behind a lasting legacy became the catalyst for Janet's next chapter. She decided to pen her memoir, a decision that would unveil a hidden talent and passion for writing. As Janet began to chronicle her life experiences, she discovered an unexpected source of joy and fulfillment in the writing process. Each page of her memoir not only captured her rich life story but brought her immense satisfaction. This newfound pleasure in writing took her by surprise, opening up a world of possibilities she had never considered.

The completion of her first book marked a significant personal achievement for Janet. However, it also served as a gateway to a new vocation. The success of her initial publication boosted her confidence, inspiring her to embark on a second book. What began as a personal project to connect with her grandchildren had blossomed into a second career as an author.

Janet Stewart's journey from culinary instructor to author stands as a powerful testament to the possibilities that retirement can offer. Her story challenges the conventional notion that retirement marks the end of productivity and creativity. Instead, it illustrates how this phase of life can be a beginning—an opportunity to explore untapped potential and pursue new passions.

Janet's experience serves as an inspiration to retirees and soon-to-be retirees. It encourages them to look beyond traditional retirement activities and embrace the chance to redefine themselves. Her journey reminds us that it's never too late to explore new avenues and that our later years can indeed be our most creatively fulfilling.

In conclusion, Janet Stewart's transition from the kitchen to the keyboard is a compelling narrative of personal growth and reinvention. It highlights the transformative power of embracing new challenges and following unexpected passions, proving that retirement can be a time of exciting new beginnings rather than an endpoint.

What's Next for You? Embracing New Passions and Possibilities

Janet Stewart's journey proves that retirement isn't about slowing down—it's about shifting gears and discovering new ways to express yourself. Her transition from culinary instructor to author is a powerful reminder that our later years can be a time of exploration, reinvention, and fulfillment.

Now, it's your turn.

* What hidden passions or talents have been waiting for you to explore?
* How can you use your life experiences to inspire, teach, or create something meaningful?
* What new adventure could you embark on that brings you joy and purpose?

Like Janet, your next chapter can be a time of creativity, learning, and personal growth—whether that means writing, painting, mentoring, traveling, or starting a completely new endeavor.

→ **Your story is still being written. What will your next chapter be?**

From Healing Hands to Captured Moments: Pam Einarsen's Journey of Rediscovery and Passion

Pam Einarsen's journey from nursing to photography is a tale of rediscovery and passion that highlights how changing careers can lead to profound personal and professional fulfillment. Pam began her career as an oncology nurse dedicated to helping patients navigate their most vulnerable moments. Her days were filled with administering chemotherapy or providing patient care, where compassion and precision were paramount. Yet, outside her shifts, Pam harbored a growing passion for photography, an art form she found both soothing and exhilarating.

The pivot in Pam's career path was sparked by a simple realization during a community photography class she attended to unwind. As she peered through the lens, she saw not just images but stories waiting to be told. Her perspective as a nurse, which had attuned her to the nuances of human emotion and condition, enriched her approach to photography. She could capture moments with a sensitivity and depth that resonated with those she photographed.

Motivated by the joy and satisfaction that came from capturing these stories, Pam decided to make a bold move. She transitioned from nursing to professional photography, founding her own business. This decision was driven not just by her love for photography but by her desire to connect with people in a different, yet still profoundly impactful, way.

As a photographer, Pam specializes in portraits and documentary-style photography, using her skills to capture the essence of her subjects. Her background in oncology nursing, with its emphasis on empathy and care, allows her to create a comfortable and trusting environment for her subjects. Pam found that being a nurse or a photographer was not that different since both help people feel comfortable in uncomfortable situations. This unique approach leads to deeply personal and expressive images that reveal the personality and spirit of the individuals she photographs.

The entrepreneurial aspect of Pam's career also brings her great joy. Running her own business offers the freedom to explore creative projects and initiatives that align with her values and artistic vision. It allows her to connect with the community on her terms, participating in local events, offering workshops, and providing mentorship to aspiring photographers.

Pam's story is a testament to the joys and rewards of following one's passion and leveraging past experiences in new ways. Her journey from oncology nursing to photography not only transformed her career but enriched her personal life, giving her a new medium through which to express her compassion, creativity, and joy in human connection. Pam loves that, in her business, each day is different and she constantly has new stories to tell. Today, she continues to inspire and influence through her lens, proving it's never too late to pursue a path that brings true joy and fulfillment.

What's Next for You? Turning Passion into Your Next Chapter

Pam Einarsen's journey reminds us that reinvention is always possible—no matter where you are in life. Her shift from oncology nursing to professional photography is proof that our skills, passions, and experiences can come together in ways we never expected, leading to greater fulfillment and deeper human connections.

Now, it's your turn.

- Is there a passion or creative pursuit you've always wanted to explore?
- How can your past experiences shape an exciting new path?
- What bold step could you take today toward a more fulfilling next chapter?

Like Pam, you have the opportunity to embrace a new passion, build something meaningful, and continue making a difference—just in a different way.

→ **Your journey is still unfolding. Where will your passion take you next?**

Summary

For teachers, retirement can feel uncertain without the familiar structure of the classroom and the daily demands of work. However, this phase of life offers a unique opportunity to rediscover purpose and create a meaningful new chapter.

Purpose doesn't have to be grand—it can be found in small, fulfilling activities that align with your values and passions. Whether it's mentoring young educators, volunteering in your community, or exploring hobbies you've long set aside, the key is to stay connected to what inspires you. For educators, purpose often lies in continuing to make a difference, even beyond the classroom. What activities or contributions would bring you joy and fulfillment in this next chapter?

Discovering your purpose can be both exhilarating and challenging, especially for teachers stepping into retirement. It's exhilarating because it opens the door to endless possibilities—you're no longer bound by the constraints of a rigid schedule or the demands of the classroom. This is your time to dream big, explore passions you may have set aside, and redefine what fulfillment looks like for you. Whether it's mentoring, volunteering, creating, or learning something entirely new, the freedom to choose your path is invigorating.

At the same time, it can be challenging because purpose doesn't always reveal itself immediately. For educators, so much of your identity has been tied to your role as a teacher, and stepping away from that can feel disorienting. It requires deep self-reflection and a willingness to try new things, even if they feel unfamiliar at first. The key is to start small—make a list of what you love to do, what excites you, and what aligns with your values. Then, explore how those passions can connect to a larger purpose, whether it's contributing to your community, pursuing a creative endeavor, or simply enriching your own life.

Remember, purpose doesn't have to be grand or world-changing. It's about finding what brings you joy and meaning, and that can be as simple as sharing your wisdom with others or dedicating time to a hobby you love. The journey to discovering your purpose is as valuable as the destination itself, and it's never too late to embrace the adventure.

Key Takeaways:
- Purpose is crucial for maintaining motivation and direction in retirement.
- Your purpose can be simple yet meaningful—what matters is that it resonates with you.
- Consider ways to align your purpose with activities that make you feel fulfilled, such as volunteering or pursuing hobbies.

Journaling Reflections

What passions or dreams are you excited to explore in this next chapter?

1. What are the activities or experiences that make you feel most alive and fulfilled? How can you incorporate more of these into your daily or weekly routine?

_____
_____
_____

2. What values guide your decisions and actions? How can you align your purpose with these core values?

_____
_____
_____

3. Think about a time when you felt a deep sense of purpose. What were you doing, and how can you replicate that experience in your current life?

_____
_____
_____

4. How do you want to contribute to the world or your community in this new chapter? What small steps can you take toward making that contribution?

_____
_____
_____

5. What does living a purposeful life mean to you, and how can you ensure your decisions reflect that purpose as you move forward?

_____
_____
_____

STEP 3
DISCOVER AND LIVE FROM YOUR STRENGTHS

DISCOVERING AND LIVING FROM YOUR STRENGTHS

"What lies behind us and what lies before us are tiny matters compared to what lies within us." — *Author Unknown*

This quote emphasizes the importance of tapping into your inner strengths as you navigate this new phase of life.

"Success is achieved by developing our strengths, not by eliminating our weaknesses." — *Marilyn vos Savant*

This quote reminds us that focusing on our strengths is key to unlocking fulfillment in our retirement years.

Discovering and Embracing Your Strengths

As teachers, you've spent years helping students uncover their strengths, but how often have you paused to reflect on your own? Peter Drucker's insight about strengths is especially relevant for educators transitioning into retirement or a "refire" stage. You may not have considered your strengths deeply before, but this is the perfect time to do so. In teaching, your strengths might include exceptional communication, creativity in lesson planning, or the ability to inspire and connect with others. These are not just skills—they are core strengths that can be applied in countless ways beyond the classroom.

Too often, we focus on fixing weaknesses rather than celebrating and building on our strengths. But your "refire" stage is the time to flip that script. Reflect on what makes you feel most capable and energized. For example, if you excelled at organizing school events, your strengths might include leadership, time management, and collaboration. If you thrived in one-on-one student mentoring, your strengths could be empathy, problem-solving, and active listening.

Remember, strengths are as varied as people are, and they often go unnoticed because they come so naturally to us. Take time to ask friends, family, or former colleagues what they see as your greatest strengths—they may highlight qualities you've overlooked. And don't forget the concept of multiple intelligences. Your strengths might lie in social intelligence, artistic intelligence, or even kinesthetic intelligence, like the ability to move and teach through physical activity.

The key is to focus on what makes you shine and brings you joy. What strengths have you relied on throughout your teaching career, and how might they guide you in this next chapter?

Our Strengths Are Our Gifts

As educators, your strengths have always been your gifts—whether it's your ability to communicate, inspire, organize, or connect with others. Think of Oprah, a natural communicator who built an entire world around her gift by nurturing and developing it. Similarly, as teachers, your strengths have shaped countless lives in the classroom. Now, as you transition into your "refire" stage, it's time to focus on those gifts in a way that adds value to your life and the lives of others.

Pursue Your Strengths with Passion

In this new chapter, let go of the weaknesses that may have been highlighted during your career. Work environments often focus on what needs "fixing," but now is the time to embrace "refire thinking." This means channeling your energy into your strengths and the dreams they inspire. What are the traits that made you a great teacher? Perhaps it's your creativity, your ability to adapt, or your knack for motivating others. These are the gifts that will guide you forward.

Retirement offers the freedom to rediscover yourself. It's a time to explore strengths that may not have been fully revealed in your teaching career. Maybe you've always had a talent for storytelling, mentoring, or even crafting. Now, with the wisdom you've gained, you can live those strengths fully and passionately. This is your time to align your gifts with your purpose and create a life that feels deeply fulfilling.

What strengths are you most excited to explore and nurture in this next phase of your journey?

Strength Discovery Exercises

Here's a simple exercise you can do to home in on your strengths. Take a sheet of paper and draw a line lengthwise down the middle. On one side, write down your hobbies. If you don't have any hobbies, write down things you would like to do. On the other side, write the strengths you employ or would need to perform those tasks well. For example, if your hobby is making jewelry, that takes dexterity, patience, creativity, an eye for design, and persistence, among other things.

Once you have completed your list of strengths, it's time to combine your strength discoveries with your purpose discoveries. Your strengths are like fuel—the driving energy that you will use to propel you toward realizing your purpose.

Additional exercises are available to help you identify your strengths. One such program is offered by the Gallup Poll, which has published the book The Strength Finder. The program provides an assessment to help you figure out your strengths. Once you've learned your strengths, strategies are given for how to nurture them. The assessments are completed online in tandem with working through the book. The program's goal is to find your top five strengths. The book is available at http://www.gallup.com/.

Leveraging My Strengths: My Journey as a Cruise Destination Presenter

Embarking on a cruise isn't just about soaking up the sun or indulging in endless buffets—it's a voyage into the heart of cultures, histories, and natural wonders. I've found a way to combine my love of teaching with my adventurous spirit, working as a cruise lecturer on luxury liners and traveling the world. This role has allowed me to blend my lifelong passion for education, my zeal for research, and my curiosity for travel into a career that's as enriching as it is exhilarating.

My presentations, which delve into the rich and often overlooked cultures of the destinations we visit, have become a highlight for many guests. Teachers and lifelong learners alike are drawn to the engaging storytelling and in-depth research I bring to each lecture, often attending every session and staying afterward to discuss more. It's a joy to see cruise guests transform into eager students, creating a classroom-like atmosphere on the ship.

From the volcanic landscapes of Hawaii to the ancient ruins of the Mediterranean, the rugged beauty of Alaska, and the vibrant rhythms of the Caribbean, my journeys have taken me to some of the most breathtaking corners of the globe. But these adventures aren't just personal escapes—they're opportunities to inspire and educate others. Each destination becomes a classroom, and every lecture is a chance to spark curiosity and deepen understanding. My skills as a teacher allow me to craft presentations that captivate and engage, weaving together the rich histories, diverse cultures, and stunning geographies of each port of call. Whether it's uncovering the secrets of ancient civilizations or sharing the best local delicacies, I transform every talk into an unforgettable learning experience.

This role is a win-win for everyone. Cruise lines benefit from offering an elevated guest experience, while passengers gain deeper insights and practical knowledge that enrich their journeys. For me, it's a dream realized—a chance to share my passion for learning and storytelling while being endlessly inspired by the enthusiasm of my audience. For other teachers, this is an extraordinary opportunity to blend their love of adventure with their strengths as educators. Imagine stepping into a role where your ability to engage, inspire, and teach transforms the travel experience for others. It's proof that teaching doesn't end in the classroom—it evolves, just like we do.

Every voyage is a step further in my journey of learning and sharing. Whether I'm unraveling the political history of a Mediterranean island or revealing the best sunset spots in Hawaii, each lecture is a celebration of discovery. Even in retirement, I've found a way to make life as expansive as the ocean horizons I sail across. What stories will you share on your next adventure? For teachers ready to embrace their strengths beyond the classroom, the possibilities are as vast as the seas.

What's Next for You? Charting a New Course with Your Strengths

My journey as a cruise destination presenter proves that teaching doesn't end in the classroom—it simply evolves. By blending my love for education, storytelling, and travel, I've discovered a career that allows me to inspire, engage, and explore the world in a meaningful way.

Now, it's your turn.

✱ How can you leverage your strengths in a new and exciting way?

✱ What passions have been calling to you that you can finally embrace?

✱ Where in the world—or in life—do you want to go next?

Like me, you have the opportunity to redefine what your next chapter looks like—whether through travel, teaching, writing, or sharing your knowledge in an unexpected way. The classroom may change, but the impact remains the same.

→ **The world is waiting. How will you share your story?**

From Badge to Pulpit: A Protector's Journey to Spiritual Service

Carleton Giles always knew he was meant to serve—a call he first answered by joining the police force. As a young officer patrolling the streets, Carleton was deeply moved by the struggles and stories of the people he encountered. His empathy and instinct for mediation earned him respect in every corner of the community. Yet, despite his commitment, he often felt that something was missing, that he was meant for another kind of service.

Years passed, and Carleton moved through various assignments, his days filled with the tangible tension of law enforcement and nights spent in quiet contemplation. The turning point came unexpectedly during a routine community meeting at a local church, where he was asked to speak about safety and cooperation. As he addressed the congregation, something within him shifted. The warmth of the gathered crowd, their attentive eyes not just looking but seeking, sparked a revelation in Carleton: His words could heal, not just command; they could offer hope, not just orders.

That night, under the soft hum of the church lights, Carleton began to feel a divine nudge, a call toward a path that may have been chasing him all along. Now he imagined a life's work he could not envision his life without. He began attending divinity school, juggling his duties as a police officer with his studies. With every scripture and sermon, Carleton found a piece of the puzzle that was his true self, feeling more at peace than he had in his entire career in law enforcement.

Getting assigned to a local congregation of his own, Carleton managed to balance a bi-vocational career as pastor and police officer. Carleton later retired from the police force, a bittersweet farewell to a significant chapter of his life, and took on a new role as head of a state public safety agency, all the while leading congregants through the labyrinth of life. Ultimately, Carleton retired and embraced his new role as a full-time preacher. He used his pulpit to bridge divides, heal old wounds, and build a community grounded in faith and mutual respect. His sermons, rich with life lessons from his police days, resonated deeply with his congregation, drawing in people from all walks of life.

Today, Reverend Carleton Giles leads a thriving church community, his days filled with outreach, counseling, and community service. His journey from police officer to preacher is a testament to the power of listening to one's inner calling and the courage to pursue it relentlessly. Carleton's story inspires many, proving it is never too late to redefine your life's work and make a difference in the world in profound new ways.

What's Next for You? Answering the Call to a New Purpose

Carleton Giles' journey reminds us that our true calling often reveals itself in unexpected ways. His path from law enforcement to ministry proves that service comes in many forms, and sometimes, the skills we develop in one career prepare us for an even greater purpose in another.

Now, it's your turn.

- ✴ Is there a passion or calling that has been nudging you toward a new direction?
- ✴ How can your past experiences shape a future of deeper meaning and impact?
- ✴ What steps can you take today to explore a purpose-driven next chapter?

Like Carleton, you have the power to transform your journey—whether that means stepping into leadership, mentoring others, or pursuing a long-held dream that has been waiting for its moment.

→ **Your next chapter is waiting to be written. How will you answer the call?**

Breaking Barriers, Changing Lives: How Celeste Mergens is Empowering Girls Around the World"

Sometimes, a single moment of awareness can ignite a global movement. For Celeste Mergens, that moment came while volunteering at an orphanage in Kenya.

She learned that young girls were missing school for days at a time—not because they lacked motivation, but because they lacked access to feminine hygiene products.

"Some of them were sitting in their rooms for days, missing school because they had no way to manage their periods," Celeste recalls. "When I brought them washable disposable products, they said: 'Thanks so much. Now we can go to school.' That was the moment Days for Girls was born."

At that moment, Celeste knew she had to do more.

She thought she was simply solving a problem for a few girls. Instead, she sparked a global movement that is changing the lives of women and girls in more than 145 countries.

What started as a small act of kindness became Days for Girls International, a nonprofit that has helped nearly a million girls stay in school, maintain their dignity, and reclaim their futures.

Since 2008, the organization has:

- Created access to sustainable, washable feminine hygiene kits for nearly 800,000 women and girls worldwide
- Built a global network of volunteers, micro-entrepreneurs, and partners in more than 145 countries
- Empowered women with entrepreneurship opportunities, allowing them to lift themselves and their families out of poverty
- Provided education and menstrual health awareness, breaking cultural taboos and giving women control over their own bodies

From New Orleans to Nepal and Uganda to Guyana, Celeste

and her team are not just providing a product—they are changing the narrative, giving women and girls a seat at the table, a voice in their communities, and a chance at a brighter future.

The work isn't just about period products—it's about dignity, education, and opportunity.

Millions of girls drop out of school because of something as natural as menstruation. Women lose work opportunities, being forced to stay home because they lack basic supplies. In many communities, talking about menstruation is taboo, leaving girls uneducated and ashamed of their own bodies.

Celeste is breaking those barriers.

"I don't go into a slum and say 'you poor, poor people,' because I know those are just circumstances," she says. "You can spend a lot of money shaming people and not get the results you seek. But when you honor their wisdom and strength, you give them a stake in the solution."

That philosophy is at the heart of Days for Girls.

Rather than simply donating supplies, they have built a microenterprise model, allowing women to manufacture and sell Days for Girls kits in their own communities. This means:

- Girls stay in school
- Women can go to work
- Families can earn an income
- Communities become self-sustaining

Celeste's biggest challenge? Getting people to believe the need for menstrual supplies was even a problem in the first place.

"At first, people could not imagine that the need for menstrual supplies could be true," she says. "Our biggest challenge now is tackling our audacious goal: helping all girls around the world."

And they are doing it—one kit, one community, one country at a time.

Scaling an initiative of this magnitude is no small feat. But Celeste refuses to let obstacles stand in the way of progress.

With a growing network of volunteers, educators, and micro-entrepreneurs, Days for Girls is on a mission to ensure that no girl has to miss school, lose opportunities, or feel ashamed because of something as natural as her period.

Celeste Mergens' story is a testament to what happens when one person refuses to accept the status quo.

She didn't wait for someone else to solve the problem. She took action.

And now, she's calling on others to do the same.

- What barriers do you see in the world that need breaking?
- How can you use your skills, time, or resources to create change?
- What small step can you take today that could spark something bigger than you ever imagined?

Like Celeste, you have the power to change lives.

→ **Take the first step. Be the change.**

Summary

This chapter is a celebration of your natural strengths—the unique gifts that make you who you are. It's an invitation to shift your focus away from fixing weaknesses and instead embrace what you do best with confidence and pride. By identifying and nurturing your strengths, you unlock the potential to create a retirement—or any new chapter of life—filled with joy, purpose, and fulfillment. This is your time to align your passions and talents with meaningful activities that energize and inspire you. When you leverage your strengths, you're not just living—you're thriving, with wisdom and freedom as your guide. What better way to step into this exciting new chapter of life?

But here's the magic: your strengths don't just benefit you—they have the power to inspire and uplift others, especially fellow teachers who may be navigating their own transitions. Imagine sharing your journey of self-discovery with other educators, showing them how to embrace their own unique gifts and passions. Whether it's through mentoring, leading workshops, or simply sharing your story, you can create a ripple effect of encouragement and empowerment.

Think about the teacher who always brought history to life with vivid storytelling or the one who had a knack for connecting with students through humor. These strengths don't fade when the classroom door closes—they evolve. By sharing how you've channeled your talents into new adventures, like becoming a cruise lecturer or writing a book, you can inspire others to see the endless possibilities that lie beyond the classroom.

This chapter isn't just about celebrating your strengths—it's about using them to build connections, spark ideas, and remind others that life after teaching can be just as impactful and rewarding. So, how will you use your gifts to inspire others and create a legacy that extends far beyond your own journey?

Discovering and Living from Your Strengths

Recognizing and living from your strengths is a transformative step toward creating a fulfilling and joyful retirement. As educators, you've spent years helping others uncover their potential—now it's your turn to focus on your own. The beauty of this new chapter is that you don't have to navigate it alone. Just as you built a community in your teaching career, you can create a supportive network to help you explore and live out your strengths.

Consider forming or joining a group of like-minded retired educators who share your passion for growth and contribution. These groups can provide encouragement, accountability, and fresh ideas as you explore new ways to use your strengths. You might also connect with local teacher unions or organizations that offer programs for retired educators, where you can share your expertise or mentor younger teachers.

If you're looking to expand your reach, think about joining online communities or forums for retired teachers. These spaces are wonderful for exchanging ideas, discovering opportunities, and finding inspiration from others who are also embracing this exciting stage of life. Whether it's through volunteering, collaborating on projects, or simply sharing stories, these connections can make your journey richer and more rewarding.

Key Takeaways:
- Identify your natural talents and embrace them in this new chapter.
- Retirement is an opportunity to shift from improving weaknesses to enhancing strengths.
- Engaging with your strengths leads to greater fulfillment and purpose.

Journaling Reflections

What kind of community or support system would inspire you most as you step into this new chapter?

What are your natural strengths—those talents or qualities that come easily to you? How have these strengths supported your success in the past, and how can they shape your future?

_____
_____
_____

1. Think of a moment when you felt truly empowered or accomplished. What strengths were you using, and how can you use those same strengths in your next chapter?

_____
_____
_____

2. What areas of your life have been more focused on improving weaknesses than leveraging strengths? How can you shift your focus to build on what you're naturally good at?

_____
_____
_____

3. Which strength do others often notice or compliment you on? How can you use this strength more intentionally in your everyday life?

_____
_____
_____

4. What are some specific ways you can bring more of your strengths into your daily activities to create more joy and fulfillment?

_____
_____
_____

STEP 4
MANAGE YOUR TIME EFFECTIVELY

EFFECTIVE TIME MANAGEMENT

"The bad news is time flies. The good news is you're the pilot." — *Michael Altshuler*

This quote underscores the importance of taking control of your time and how you spend it in this new chapter.

"Don't count the days. Make the days count."
— *Muhammad Ali*

This quote reminds us to ensure that every day is spent in a way that brings purpose and fulfillment.

Time Management and Purpose

As a teacher, you've spent your career with structured days, clear goals, and a deep sense of purpose. Transitioning into retirement can feel liberating, but it also presents a unique challenge: how to fill those extra seven to nine hours each day in a way that feels meaningful. While financial planning is often the focus before retirement, it's equally important to plan for how you'll use your time and energy to maintain a sense of fulfillment and purpose.

Freedom in retirement is a gift, but it comes with responsibility—responsibility to yourself to stay engaged, purposeful, and balanced. Without a plan, it's easy to drift or feel untethered. That's why time management becomes the bridge between your strengths, purpose, and daily life. It's not about rigid schedules but about intentionally crafting your days to reflect your values and passions.

Variety is key. While it's tempting to focus on one activity, like golfing or reading, true fulfillment often comes from a mix of pursuits. Consider blending recreation with activities that tap into your teaching strengths—mentoring younger educators, volunteering in your community, or even writing a book to share your wisdom. These activities not only keep your days dynamic but they ensure you're contributing in ways that align with your purpose.

Lifelong Learning: Mastering Time Management in Retirement for Teachers

As a teacher, you've spent your life fostering learning in others—now it's your turn to embrace lifelong learning as a way to enrich your retirement. Exploring new skills and interests not only keeps your mind sharp but provides structure and purpose to your days. Whether it's diving deeper into hobbies you love or pursuing entirely new passions, lifelong education is a powerful tool for self-discovery and fulfillment.

Community education programs, like those offered by local colleges or Osher Lifelong Learning Institutes (OLLI), are fantastic options. These programs are often affordable, designed for retirees, and come with built-in schedules, giving your days a sense of rhythm and focus. For example, if you've always loved the arts, why not take a painting or photography class? Or, if technology feels like a gap, now is the perfect time to build your confidence with computer skills. Competence in new areas leads to confidence, which opens doors to even more opportunities for joy and growth.

It's also important to recognize what doesn't interest you. For instance, if you're not drawn to the technical side of things, like building a website, consider outsourcing those tasks while focusing on learning skills that excite you. This balance allows you to stay energized and engaged while avoiding unnecessary frustration.

To make the most of your time, consider keeping an Activity Log. Tracking how you spend your days and noting your energy levels can reveal when you're most productive and when you need rest. This insight helps you optimize your schedule, ensuring you focus on meaningful activities during your peak hours.

What new skills or interests are you most excited to explore in this next chapter?

How to Make an Activity Log

To create an Activity Log, without making any changes in your daily behavior, make a note of each activity you perform as it's done. In addition, make a note of your mood and energy level when you move from one undertaking to the next.

Your log should include even the most trivial things. Every time you switch from one activity to the next, whether checking email, taking a walk, making a meal, or gossiping on the phone, note the change and the time.

Why Keep an Activity Log?

1. Create Structure and Purpose

The shift from a structured work life to the freedom of retirement can be disorienting. An activity log provides a framework to build a routine and instill purpose in your days. This sense of structure is essential for mental and emotional well-being, ensuring your retirement is as meaningful as it is enjoyable.

2. Maximize Time Management

With the gift of more free time, it's easy to lose track of hours and feel aimless. An activity log lets you evaluate how you spend your time, helping you focus on activities that align with your goals, passions, and values.

3. Prioritize Health and Wellness

Staying physically active is crucial for health in later years. By tracking your exercise habits in an activity log, you can stay accountable to your fitness goals, monitor progress, and identify opportunities to add more movement to your routine.

4. Stimulate Cognitive Growth

Engaging in mentally stimulating activities, like learning a new skill or pursuing a hobby, helps maintain cognitive health. An activity log encourages you to incorporate intellectually enriching activities and provides a way to track your development.

5. Maintain Social Connections

Retirement can sometimes lead to reduced social engagement, but an activity log can help you balance your calendar with opportunities for connection. Regularly noting social activities ensures you're nurturing relationships and avoiding isolation.

How to Keep an Activity Log

1. Choose a Format That Suits You

Decide whether you prefer a physical notebook, a digital app, or a simple spreadsheet. The most important factor is choosing a format you'll use consistently.

2. Organize by Categories

Divide your activities into key categories like:

- Physical Exercise
- Social Engagements
- Hobbies and Recreation
- Self-Development
- Leisure and Relaxation

This structure allows for a clearer picture of how you're balancing different aspects of your life.

3. Record Your Daily Activities

Develop a daily habit of logging activities. For each entry, include:

- Date and time
- Activity description
- Duration
- Your feelings during and after the activity
- Any notable outcomes or insights

4. Be Detailed and Consistent

Consistency is key! Aim to record your activities at the same time each day, and provide as much detail as possible to make your log a helpful resource for reflection.

5. Reflect and Adjust Regularly

Review your log weekly or monthly to identify patterns, celebrate achievements, and pinpoint areas for improvement. Adjust your plans to ensure you're living in alignment with your goals and values.

You can customize the columns or categories to include specific details like emotional state, social interactions, or health goals. Logging consistently helps you analyze patterns and adjust your routine for a fulfilling retirement.

By keeping an activity log, you're not just tracking time—you're designing a life filled with purpose, joy, and balance. Whether it's discovering new passions, improving health, or staying connected with loved ones, your activity log can be a powerful tool for creating your best retirement chapter.

Learning from Your Log

After keeping an Activity Log for a few days, you will begin to see exactly how your time is, or isn't, being managed, plus how much time you have spent productively and how much time you have frittered away or "wasted."

Other patterns will also emerge as you analyze your Activity Log.

For example, you may engage in certain activities when you have higher energy levels and a more pleasant mood, and descend to time-wasting activities when your energy or mood falls low. You may take breaks at certain points, but feel recharged at other points.

In fact, you will see how much the nature and quality of your daily regimen depends on the amount and quality of your rest periods, the amount and quality of your mealtimes, and the extent to which you take care of yourself in general. The importance of having this knowledge is then being able to experiment with various factors to see how your productivity fluctuates.

Finally, when analyzing your Activity Log, you must pose several questions to yourself to extract the important information you will need when reshaping your time:

- Which areas take up the most and least of your time?
- How does your current Activity Log compare with how it may have looked five, ten, twenty, or thirty years ago?
- How did you handle shifts in scheduling or time management at other times in your life?

If this page does not allow sufficient space for your answers to any question, continue your responses in your journal.

Key Benefits of Your Activity Log

Your Activity Log is a useful graphic aid in helping you to see both how you spend your time and how to become proactive in making changes where needed to make the most of your time.

Your Activity Log helps you structure your time around your priorities. If your priority is family, but you see you're only devoting three hours a week to that priority, then you know you can significantly increase that number by making changes to your schedule. This ties directly back into fulfilling your purpose.

Conversely, your Activity Log helps you determine what you're spending too much time on and, therefore, what you need to delegate out or eliminate altogether.

In reviewing your Activity Log, you can position yourself to take on new challenges as you feel more able to surmount them. If your purpose is to spend more time servicing the community, then adding new activities as you feel ready to do so can be simply a matter of adding new things to your Activity Log and then following through. An Activity Log is a self-determined guide in your endeavors.

When a woman I know started to use an Activity Log, she realized that although she considered her family a top priority, she was spending very little time with them. She always had an excuse for why she couldn't visit. The Activity Log helped her align her priorities with her schedule, and she started to make time to visit each of her children regularly, although they lived some distance away.

As teachers, you've mastered the art of planning and time management in the classroom. Now, in retirement, an Activity Log can become your personal roadmap to ensure your time aligns with your priorities and purpose. By keeping an Activity Log for just a few days, you'll gain a clear picture of how your time is being spent—both productively and unproductively—and uncover patterns that can guide you toward a more fulfilling daily routine.

Your Activity Log is more than just a time tracker—it's a powerful visual aid that helps you align your schedule with your values.

This tool also empowers you to take on new challenges as you feel ready. Whether it's volunteering, learning a new skill, or pursuing a passion project, your Activity Log helps you see where and how to integrate these activities into your life. It's a guide to living your purpose with intention and clarity.

What patterns or priorities do you think your Activity Log might reveal about your time?

The Happiness Legacy: How Lionel Ketchian is Spreading Joy and Purpose

Lionel Ketchian isn't just a retiree; he's a beacon of joy in a world that often forgets the simple power of being happy. Since stepping away from his traditional career path in 1983, Lionel has dedicated his life to a mission that transcends the typical retirement pastime: Teaching others that happiness is not just a fleeting moment but a conscious choice that can be cultivated and maintained.

Lionel's journey into the world of happiness didn't begin in quiet solitude but as a vibrant sharing of insights and wisdom. He is the charismatic cohost of the weekly cable television program The Happiness Show, where he explores various aspects of happiness, from everyday tips to profound life changes that can increase emotional well-being. The show has become a cornerstone for many looking for consistent, positive messages in their weekly routine.

In addition to his television presence, Lionel continues to make a difference in his local community through his written words. As the author of the Be Happy Zone column in the Fairfield Citizen-News, he regularly pens articles that provide readers with practical advice on nurturing and sustaining happiness in their lives. His column has not only enriched his readers' lives but become a staple of positivity in the newspaper.

Beyond his roles in broadcasting and journalism, Lionel is also the esteemed author of Food for Thought—a book filled with inspirational words of wisdom that has garnered praise and endorsements from such notable figures as Rev. Norman Vincent Peale and Ken Blanchard. This book compiles Lionel's reflections on happiness and practical philosophy, offering readers nourishing mental insights that support a joyful life.

Lionel's commitment to spreading happiness extends into interactive experiences. He has spent decades hosting seminars and workshops, where he engages directly with individuals eager to learn how to live more joyfully. His teachings emphasize that happiness is a choice available to everyone, regardless of their circumstances. Through these sessions, he has empowered hundreds, perhaps even thousands, to take active steps toward a happier existence.

What sets Lionel apart is his unwavering belief in happiness as a fundamental right and achievable state for everyone. His work over the years has not only changed individual lives but influenced community perspectives on mental health and well-being. His approachable methods and enduring enthusiasm make him a respected and beloved figure in the field of happiness education.

Lionel Ketchian's post-retirement life is a testament to how one can use their time and talents to truly make a difference in the world. Not only has he found personal joy, but he has multiplied it by sharing it with others, proving that retirement can be the most active and inspiring chapter of one's life.

What's Next for You? Choosing Joy and Purpose in Your Next Chapter

Lionel Ketchian's journey is proof that retirement isn't about stepping back—it's about stepping into a life of purpose and impact. His mission to spread happiness reminds us that joy is not just something we experience; it's something we can create and share with the world.

Now, it's your turn.

✴ What passion or message do you feel called to share?

✴ How can you use your time and talents to uplift and inspire others?

✴ What small steps can you take today to create a more meaningful and joyful next chapter?

Like Lionel, you have the power to redefine what retirement means—whether that's through teaching, writing, speaking, or simply being a beacon of positivity for those around you.

→ **Happiness is a choice. How will you use your next chapter to spread joy?**

Purposeful Moments: How Joyce Cohen and Vicki Thomas Use Their Time in Retirement

Joyce Cohen and Vicki Thomas are prime examples of retirees who choose to spend their time in purposeful and meaningful ways. Despite enjoying successful careers and extensive networks that could easily have led them to a leisurely retirement, they instead chose a path of continued contribution and innovation. In their seventies, they pooled their talents, experience, and wisdom to establish My Future Purpose, LLC (MFP), a company dedicated to helping individuals transition from their careers and discover what's next.

Originally, MFP planned to host conferences featuring keynote speakers, authors, and panelists to explore career transitions and what lies beyond. However, the advent of COVID-19 required a swift pivot. Recognizing the growing need for community during these homebound times, Joyce and Vicki initiated Pause for Purpose, a bimonthly virtual discussion group that quickly became a cornerstone of the organization, accessible to everyone.

Today, My Future Purpose is a thriving entity that offers a diverse range of services, including virtual and on-site workshops, retreats, member benefits, and one-on-one coaching, all designed to help individuals rediscover their purpose and direction in life. The MFP team is equipped to explore purpose in a broad context or help individuals develop a focused plan of action.

Vicki Thomas, now the Chief Purpose Officer, won the $100,000 Purpose Prize in 2013 from Encore.org for using her expertise to help veteran nonprofits gain recognition by securing national and local media coverage for veterans needing housing solutions. As Chief Relationship Officer, Joyce Cohen, a career development specialist, leverages her extensive experience to help people find their future direction. She has facilitated hundreds of workshops worldwide, focusing on career development, mid-life transition, and engagement, emphasizing renewed purpose.

Joyce's leadership extended through her presidency at the Life Planning Network from 2015 to 2020, where she helped achieve non-profit designation and created impactful programs like Paired2Learn. Her contributions continue as she serves on the National Board and is actively involved in internal projects.

Both Joyce and Vicki have left indelible marks on their fields and continue to inspire others by demonstrating that retirement can be a dynamic stage of life rich with opportunities for growth and impact. They are driven by a shared belief, inspired by George Bernard Shaw: "I want to be all used up when I die...this is a splendid torch I have hold of, and I want to make it burn as brightly as possible before passing it on to future generations." Today, they are doing just that, helping others find their passion and purpose, ensuring their own torches burn bright and clear.

Summary

For teachers, retirement brings a wealth of free time—a stark contrast to the structured days of lesson plans and classroom schedules. This chapter emphasizes the importance of managing that time intentionally to create a fulfilling and purposeful retirement. By building structure into your days, you can ensure your activities align with your values and goals, just as you once aligned your teaching with your students' needs.

The key is to embrace variety. Balance recreational pursuits with activities that draw on your strengths as an educator, such as mentoring, volunteering, or even learning new skills. This diversity not only keeps your days dynamic but helps you maintain a sense of purpose and contribution.

The activity log is your tool for crafting a retirement that reflects who you are and what you value most. How will you use your time to continue making an impact, even beyond the classroom?

Key Takeaways:

✶ Time management is essential for turning free hours into fulfilling activities.

✶ Diversify your daily routine through engaging in hobbies, learning opportunities, and meaningful activities.

✶ Use tools like an Activity Log to optimize your time and ensure it aligns with your priorities.

Journaling Reflections

Time is one of your most precious resources, especially in retirement. Reflecting on how you spend it and how to create a more purposeful daily routine is essential. But here's the good news—you don't have to figure it out alone. As teachers, you've always thrived in a community, and that same sense of connection can guide you in retirement.

Start by reaching out to fellow retired educators. Many teacher unions and organizations offer programs, workshops, or even social groups specifically for retirees. These are excellent opportunities to share experiences, exchange ideas, and support one another as you navigate this new chapter. You might also consider forming a small group of retired teachers in your area to meet regularly for coffee, book discussions, or even collaborative projects like volunteering or mentoring younger educators.

Online communities are another fantastic way to stay connected. Platforms like Facebook often have groups for retired teachers where you can find inspiration, advice, and camaraderie. You could also explore professional associations or alumni networks that align with your interests—many of these groups welcome retirees and offer ways to stay involved.

As you reflect on your time, ask yourself: How can I use my strengths to contribute to my community? What activities bring me the most joy and fulfillment? And how can I connect with others to make this journey even more rewarding? Remember, retirement isn't a solo adventure—it's an opportunity to build new connections and rediscover the power of community. What kind of group or activity would make you feel most supported and inspired?

How do you currently spend your time? Does it align with the things that matter most to you? What adjustments could you make to create more meaningful moments?

_____
_____
_____

1. What activities in your day leave you feeling energized and fulfilled, and which ones drain you? How can you create more space for the energizing activities?

_____
_____
_____

2. What small, practical steps can you take to bring more structure and purpose into your day without sacrificing flexibility or joy?

_____
_____
_____

3. How can you use an Activity Log to track how you spend your time, and what patterns might you notice after doing so?

_____
_____
_____

STEP 5
STAY CONNECTED

REMAINING CONNECTED

"Alone we can do so little; together we can do so much."
— *Helen Keller*

This quote highlights the importance of connection and collaboration in creating a fulfilling retirement.

"Connection is why we're here; it is what gives purpose and meaning to our lives." — *Brené Brown*

This quote reinforces that meaningful relationships are at the heart of a purposeful life.

The Power of Connection

Retirement isn't just about stepping away from the classroom; it's a chance to strengthen and expand the relationships that enrich your life. As teachers, you've spent years building connections—with students, colleagues, and your community. Now, it's time to nurture those bonds and create new ones to ensure your retirement is as fulfilling as your career.

Maintaining old relationships is key. Think about the coworkers you've shared countless conversations with over coffee or the friends and family you've supported from afar during your busy teaching years. Retirement offers the perfect opportunity to reconnect. Schedule regular meetups, plan reunions, or simply pick up the phone to check in. For those relationships that have shifted—like with a spouse or partner—be proactive. Set aside time to rediscover each other and establish new routines that work for both of you.

Equally important is forging new connections. Joining clubs, taking classes, or volunteering are fantastic ways to meet like-minded individuals. Many retired teachers find joy in mentoring younger educators, participating in book clubs, or even traveling with new friends. If you're unsure where to start, look to your local community for programs, activities, or groups that align with your interests.

And remember, you're not alone in this journey. Many retired teachers are navigating the same transitions and looking for ways to stay connected. Reach out to teacher unions, alumni networks, or online communities for retirees. These spaces can provide support, camaraderie, and inspiration as you build this new chapter of your life.

What relationships or activities are you most excited to focus on in retirement?

Caring for Old Relationships

One of my clients recently told me that one of the toughest parts of retirement for him was the social transition because he found it difficult to make new connections. Even his relationship with his wife became difficult because she was accustomed to running the household, but now, here he was, retired and suddenly at home all the time, and she didn't want him butting in or changing anything.

He also found that when he went out and tried to socialize, he had nothing to talk about. He was really shocked how much work it takes to maintain and develop new connections with people.

He realized that, before retirement, when both husband and wife worked, you said good morning in the morning and good evening in the evening, and there may not have been a whole lot of communication. But once you retire, there's a whole different scenario. From the way my client portrayed how he and his wife felt, it was like having a stranger in the house.

In fact, with relationships you've already formed, even in marriages, you sometimes have to get to know a person all over again. This is not only because you weren't in one another's company for as many hours as you are now, but because now the contexts have shifted: children are gone, new habits are being established, and people are changing.

Again, be proactive; in this case, set parameters for getting to know one another again. Research confirms that divorce rates increase after retirement among couples who have been married for quite some time because the transitions are so difficult. Knowing this ahead of time and making preparations will offset potential problems.

In addition to attending to your existing relationships, you are in a position to forge new relationships. Your hobbies and activities can be an entry-point into this arena. Taking classes, joining activity-based clubs, or forming coalitions of like-minded individuals can lead you down new avenues of social contact.

Retirement offers teachers a unique opportunity to step out of the familiar school environment and embrace new relationships that can enrich this exciting chapter of life. Meeting new people and building friendships isn't just about filling time—it's about discovering fresh perspectives, exploring shared passions, and creating a support network that keeps you energized and connected. For teachers, who are naturally skilled at building rapport and fostering connections, this is a chance to use those strengths in a whole new way.

One of the most rewarding aspects of retirement is how new relationships can open doors to opportunities you might not have noticed before. Whether it's joining a local book club, volunteering at a community center, or attending workshops tailored to your interests, these connections can help you learn more about yourself and others. For single retirees especially, nurturing a network of friends outside of the job is essential to prevent isolation and loneliness. Consider reaching out to fellow retired teachers—they'll understand your experiences and may share your desire to stay engaged and active.

To stay connected, explore opportunities that align with your passions. Host a workshop at your local library, join a writing group to share your stories, or even collaborate with other retired educators to create events that inspire lifelong learning. You could also look into community programs or travel groups that cater to retirees, offering a blend of adventure and camaraderie. For teachers, the classroom may have been your world, but now the world can become your classroom—filled with people eager to connect, share, and grow alongside you.

How will you use your natural ability to connect and inspire to build meaningful relationships in this new phase of life? The possibilities are endless, and the rewards are immeasurable.

If you would like to make new friends, reach out. Here are a few additional ways to expand your social horizons:

- Involve yourself with projects that entail regular contact with others.
- Look into the social options available in your community and take advantage of programs and services offered at community centers.
- Seek out like-minded people through involvement in church, clubs, hospital foundations, and non-profit organizations.
- Volunteer your time and energy toward a cause near and dear to you.
- Pursue hobbies, old or new, in a place where others are doing the same.
- Find yourself an animal companion, like a dog, and walk with your new friend in areas where other dog-owners are walking their companions.
- Get back in touch with old friends, local and distant.
- Look into traveling with age-based groups.

Retirement is a significant transition, and for teachers, it can feel especially daunting to step out of the structured, familiar environment of the classroom and into the unknown. Establishing new relationships during this time can be challenging, especially when fear of rejection or feelings of being overwhelmed creep in. But just as you encouraged your students to take things one step at a time, the same wisdom applies here. Start small—perhaps it's signing up for a local class, attending a community event, or even reaching out to a fellow retired teacher for coffee. Each step builds momentum, and before you know it, you'll find yourself forming meaningful connections.

It's perfectly normal to feel hesitant. You might even catch yourself thinking, "I've spent my life teaching others—why is this so hard for me?" But remember, every new adventure begins with baby steps. Just as you guided your students through challenges, it's okay to seek a little guidance yourself. Whether it's a friend, a coach, or even a family member, don't hesitate to lean on someone who can nudge you forward and celebrate those first steps with you.

The key here is choice. In retirement, every action you take is a decision to shape your future. You can choose to embrace this new chapter with curiosity and courage, or you can let fear and stubbornness hold you back. Teachers are natural contributors—you've spent your life making a difference. Now, it's about channeling that energy into new relationships and opportunities that bring you joy and fulfillment. What's one small step you can take today to start building the connections that will enrich your life?

Building Bridges: The Power of Connections through Volunteering

After retiring from a thirty-five-year career in education, Louise initially found herself missing the daily interactions and the sense of purpose that teaching provided. Realizing she needed to fill this gap and make productive use of her time, she turned to her local library—a place that had always felt like a second home to her. The library was seeking volunteers to help in their new children's literacy program, which aimed to enhance reading skills among struggling young readers. Seeing an opportunity to leverage her teaching skills, Louise signed up as a volunteer.

A Day in the Life of a Volunteer

Louise's volunteering routine involves two mornings each week where she works one-on-one with children ages six to ten. Her sessions are carefully planned, incorporating a mix of reading aloud, discussion, and interactive activities designed to engage the children and foster a love of reading. Louise uses her educational background to assess each child's reading level and tailors her approach to meet their individual needs.

One of Louise's greatest joys in volunteering is the connections she forms with the children. Each child comes to her with unique interests, and she takes the time to learn about their hobbies, favorite books, and school activities. These details allow Louise to recommend and select reading materials that cater to each child's interests, making the reading sessions both enjoyable and effective.

Beyond her direct interactions with the children, Louise has also become a well-known figure among parents and library staff. She shares insights with parents about their children's progress and offers advice on how to encourage reading at home. The library staff appreciate her dependable presence and her contributions to enhancing their services.

Volunteering has significantly benefited Louise's life, providing her with a routine, a sense of purpose, and fulfillment that she missed after retiring. It has also allowed her to stay mentally active and engaged with the community, helping to bridge the generational gap by interacting with younger generations.

For the community, Louise's efforts contribute to improving literacy rates among children, which is a crucial foundation for their academic and personal growth. Her dedication not only supports the library's mission but fosters a culture of volunteering and community service in the area.

Louise often reflects on her volunteering as a continuation of her teaching career, but in a more flexible and less stressful environment. She enjoys the freedom to focus solely on the children's reading without the additional administrative pressures that came with teaching. Louise feels this chapter of her life is about giving back and sharing her love for literature, and she takes great satisfaction in seeing the children develop their abilities and discover new worlds through books.

In summary, Louise's story illustrates the profound impact volunteering can have in retirement. It shows that by leveraging one's professional skills and interests, any retiree can find meaningful ways to contribute to their community while enriching their own life. For Louise, volunteering at the library is not just a way to pass time; it's a vital part of her life that brings joy, purpose, and a sense of continuity from her professional career into her retirement.

What's Next for You? Finding Purpose Through Giving Back

Louise's journey proves that retirement doesn't mean leaving behind your passions—it means finding new ways to share them. By stepping into a volunteer role that aligned with her expertise and love for learning, she found a renewed sense of purpose, connection, and fulfillment.

Now, it's your turn.

* What skills or passions do you have that could benefit others?
* How can you stay engaged and make a meaningful impact in your community?
* What small step can you take today to explore volunteering, mentoring, or sharing your expertise?

Like Louise, you have the power to shape your next chapter in a way that is rewarding and impactful—whether through volunteering, teaching, mentoring, or supporting a cause close to your heart.

→ **Your next act is waiting. How will you use your time to inspire and uplift others?**

Summary

Retirement brings significant social adjustments, but staying connected is absolutely essential to maintaining emotional well-being and a sense of purpose. This chapter dives into the importance of nurturing the relationships you already have, forming new ones, and actively engaging with your community to avoid the pitfalls of isolation. For teachers, who are used to the daily interactions and camaraderie of the classroom, this transition can feel especially challenging—but it's also an opportunity to build a new kind of social network that aligns with your evolving interests and goals.

Nurturing existing relationships means taking the time to reconnect with friends and family you may have lost touch with during your busy teaching years. A simple phone call, a coffee date, or even a shared hobby can reignite those bonds. At the same time, forming new relationships can open doors to unexpected opportunities. Consider joining local groups, such as book clubs, volunteer organizations, or even retired teacher associations, where you can meet like-minded individuals who share your passions.

Engaging with your community is another powerful way to stay connected. Whether it's mentoring younger teachers, offering workshops, or volunteering at local schools, your wealth of experience can make a meaningful impact. Plus, these activities keep you active and involved, providing a sense of fulfillment and belonging.

Remember, staying connected isn't just about avoiding loneliness—it's about creating a vibrant, supportive network that enriches your life and allows you to continue making a difference. What steps will you take today to nurture your relationships and build new connections?

Key Takeaways:

- Actively nurture relationships that matter and rekindle old connections.
- Form new bonds through shared activities, hobbies, or community involvement.
- Stay connected to enhance emotional well-being and prevent isolation in retirement.

Journaling Reflections

As you embrace this transformative phase of life, remember that nurturing relationships is key—not just for your emotional well-being, but for staying inspired and engaged. For teachers, who have spent their careers fostering connections with students, parents, and colleagues, retirement is the perfect time to build a new kind of network. Reaching out to fellow educators, especially those who are also navigating retirement, can be incredibly rewarding. Who better to understand your experiences, challenges, and passions than someone who has walked a similar path?

Start by reconnecting with former colleagues. A simple coffee date or a shared activity like attending a workshop or conference can reignite those bonds. You might even consider joining retired teacher associations or local education-focused groups. These spaces are not only great for socializing but for brainstorming ways to continue making an impact—whether it's through mentoring, volunteering, or collaborating on projects that support the next generation of educators.

If you're feeling hesitant, remember that every connection starts with a single step. Send that email, make that phone call, or attend that first meeting. You've spent your life encouraging others to take risks and grow—now it's your turn to embrace this new adventure. By reaching out to other educators, you'll not only build meaningful relationships but also create opportunities to share your wisdom, learn from others, and continue contributing to the world in a way that feels fulfilling.

What's one small step you can take today to connect with a fellow educator and start building your new network?

Who in your life have you lost touch with but would like to reconnect with?

What steps can you take to rebuild that relationship?
_____
_____

1. What new communities, groups, or social activities excite you? How can you start becoming more involved in these circles to build new connections?
_____
_____

2. How do you currently stay connected with loved ones, and are there any ways you'd like to improve or expand those connections?
_____
_____

3. What role does being part of a community play in your overall happiness and fulfillment? How can you ensure that community remains an integral part of your life?
_____
_____
_____

STEP 6
REMAIN MENTALLY AND PHYSICALLY SHARP

STAYING MENTALLY AND PHYSICALLY SHARP

"Age is no barrier. It's a limitation you put on your mind."
— *Jackie Joyner-Kersee*

This quote reminds us that staying mentally and physically sharp removes the limitations we place on ourselves with age.

"I have no fear of aging, but I have a fear of boredom."
— *Penélope Cruz*

This quote underscores the importance of staying engaged and active, both mentally and physically, to live fully.

Staying Sharp: The Key to Thriving in a World of Endless Possibilities

In today's age of innovation, information, and boundless choices, staying sharp mentally and physically is more crucial than ever. With constant demands on our focus, concentration, and ability to evaluate incoming information, thriving requires us to be alert and adaptable. At the heart of this adaptability lies the ultimate foundation of a fulfilling life: maintaining mental and physical sharpness.

Without mental clarity and physical vitality, all other ambitions fade into the background. They are the fuel for energy, resilience, and the capacity to fully embrace life's opportunities. Time Magazine recently emphasized the importance of staying sharp, highlighting research that shows how prioritizing mental and physical health can significantly enhance not only longevity but our quality of life.

A Story of Renewal and Resilience

Meet Susan, a sixty-two-year-old retired teacher. When Susan stepped away from her demanding career, she initially enjoyed the newfound freedom of retirement. However, after a few months, she began to feel unmotivated and lethargic. Her days blurred together, and she felt her sharpness slipping away.

Determined not to let herself fade into inactivity, Susan decided to make changes. She started with small, manageable habits. Every morning, she solved a crossword puzzle while sipping her coffee. Not only did this mentally stimulate her, but it gave her a sense of accomplishment before the day even began.

Susan paired her mental exercises with physical activity. Each afternoon, she took a thirty-minute walk around her neighborhood. Over time, those walks became an opportunity to connect with others because she often greeted neighbors or walked with friends. Feeling more confident, Susan joined a local yoga class to improve her balance and flexibility.

By the end of her first year of this routine, Susan felt like a new person. Her energy levels soared, she slept better, and her sharpness returned. The combination of mental and physical activity helped her rediscover a sense of purpose and joy. Today, Susan often tells her friends, "You can't pour from an empty cup—taking care of yourself is the greatest gift you can give to the people and things you love."

What's Next for You? Embracing Renewal and Growth

Susan's journey is a reminder that retirement isn't the end—it's an opportunity for renewal, self-care, and rediscovery. By taking small but intentional steps, she transformed her routine, regained her energy, and found a renewed sense of purpose.

Now, it's your turn.

- ✶ How can you incorporate new habits that energize your mind and body?
- ✶ What activities bring you joy and a sense of accomplishment?
- ✶ Who can you connect with to make this next chapter more fulfilling?

Like Susan, you have the power to shape your retirement into a time of growth, connection, and vitality—whether that means learning new skills, prioritizing your health, or building meaningful relationships.

→ **Your best years are still ahead. How will you make the most of them?**

The Science Behind Staying Sharp

Research supports Susan's journey. Studies show that keeping mentally and physically active nourishes the brain, reduces the risk of cognitive decline, and boosts overall mental well-being. Physical activity does more than improve muscle tone—it releases endorphins, reduces stress, and enhances brain function. The mind-body connection is undeniable, and investing in both yields incredible results.

Practical Activities to Stay Sharp

1. Mental Fitness Activities

- **Puzzles and Brain Games:** Crosswords, Sudoku, or logic puzzles challenge your mind and improve problem-solving skills.
- **Learning Something New:** Take up a new hobby, like learning a language, playing an instrument, or exploring a creative skill such as painting.
- **Reading and Writing:** Reading books, engaging in thoughtful discussions, or journaling can deepen your thinking and sharpen your focus.

2. Physical Fitness Activities

- **Walking or Hiking:** A simple daily walk boosts cardiovascular health, improves mood, and offers time for reflection or connection.
- **Strength Training:** Resistance exercises, even with light weights, help build muscle and maintain bone density as you age.
- **Yoga or Tai Chi:** These practices improve balance, flexibility, and mental clarity through mindful movement and breathwork.

3. *Combination Activities*
   - **Dance Classes:** Dancing combines physical movement with learning and social interaction, making it an excellent choice for brain and body health.
   - **Gardening:** This low-impact activity promotes physical exercise while offering mental relaxation and focus.
   - **Volunteering:** Engaging in community service provides mental stimulation, purpose, and social connection.

The Benefits of Staying Sharp

Investing in your mental and physical sharpness pays dividends. You'll experience:

- Increased self-esteem and confidence.
- Reduced anxiety and stress.
- Better mood and resilience to life's challenges.
- Improved cognitive function and memory.
- Slowed bone loss and enhanced overall health.

The possibilities of this stage of life are endless, but they all rest on your ability to stay sharp. By nurturing your mind and body, you unlock greater joy, purpose, and vitality—ensuring you thrive in a world full of opportunity.

Susan's story reminds us it's never too late to embrace the habits that keep us sharp. Start small, be consistent, and watch how these simple changes can transform your life.

My Journey to a Sharper Mind

As I reflect on my life, I realize that maintaining a sharp mind has been a continuous journey, one that I've cultivated through a combination of hobbies, lifestyle choices, and a commitment to lifelong learning. For me, the foundation of this journey is rooted in a deep love for reading, writing, and embracing nature. Additionally, my role as a cruise lecturer has become a significant part of this journey, as it allows me to delve into fascinating research and share my findings with others.

Reading has always been my sanctuary. It allows me to explore new worlds, learn about diverse cultures, and expand my understanding of the world. Whether it's fiction or nonfiction, each book I read enriches my mind with new ideas and perspectives. This habit not only keeps my mind active but also inspires creativity and curiosity.

Writing is another essential part of my routine. It helps me process my thoughts, reflect on my experiences, and express myself in a meaningful way. Whether it's journaling, writing short stories, or even just jotting down notes, this practice keeps my mind sharp by forcing me to articulate my thoughts clearly and concisely.

Nature has a profound impact on my mental clarity. Taking daily walks outdoors allows me to connect with the natural world, breathe fresh air, and clear my mind. These walks often become moments of introspection, where I can reflect on my life, set goals, and find peace. Being in nature reminds me of the beauty and simplicity of life, which helps maintain a balanced perspective.

My commitment to a healthy lifestyle is deeply intertwined with my mental well-being. I've found that refraining from sugar and flour significantly improves my mental clarity and focus. These dietary choices not only support my physical health but enhance my cognitive function, allowing me to stay alert and engaged throughout the day.

Maintaining a normal body weight is also crucial for me. It gives me the energy to pursue my passions without feeling weighed down or lethargic. This physical well-being translates into mental vitality, enabling me to tackle challenges with enthusiasm and resilience.

As a cruise lecturer, I have the privilege of traveling to various destinations around the world. However, it's not just the travel that excites me; it's the research that precedes each journey. Delving into the history, culture, and geography of each port is a true delight. Finding new information and uncovering hidden gems brings me immense joy and feeds my curiosity. This process of discovery not only sharpens my mind but enriches my lectures, allowing me to share engaging stories and insights with my audience.

Whether I'm exploring the ancient ruins of the Mediterranean, the vibrant cities of Asia, or the breathtaking landscapes of South America, each destination offers a wealth of knowledge waiting to be uncovered. The act of researching and learning about these places keeps my mind active and engaged, as I continually seek to deepen my understanding and find new ways to connect the dots between history, culture, and contemporary life.

I believe in being a lifelong learner, always seeking opportunities to grow and expand my knowledge. In today's fast-paced world, staying updated with new technologies is essential. I make it a point to learn new skills and keep up with the latest advancements in technology. Doing so not only keeps my mind sharp but opens doors to new experiences and connections.

Whether it's learning to use new software, understanding emerging trends, or simply staying curious about how technology can improve my life, I find joy in the process of discovery. This mindset helps me stay adaptable and engaged, ensuring my mind remains active and responsive to new challenges.

My journey to maintaining a sharp mind is a holistic one, combining intellectual pursuits with physical and mental well-being. Through reading, writing, nature walks, healthy eating, research for my cruise lectures, and a commitment to lifelong learning, I've found a balance that enhances my quality of life. Each day, I feel more energized, more focused, and more ready to embrace whatever life brings. This path has taught me that a healthy lifestyle isn't just about physical health; it's about nurturing a mind that is curious, creative, and always ready to grow.

Now, it's your moment to shine.

- How will you keep your mind sharp in this exciting next chapter of your life?
- What strategies will you employ to enhance your mental and physical agility?
- What's one small action you can take today to stay sharp and vibrant?
- The path is yours to take. How will you ignite your spark and shine even brighter?

Summary

This chapter emphasizes the importance of maintaining mental and physical sharpness in retirement—a goal that resonates deeply with teachers who have spent their careers fostering growth and learning in others. Now, it's your turn to focus on yourself by embracing continuous learning, physical activity, and a balanced lifestyle to stay vibrant, active, and healthy. One fantastic way to combine physical activity with social connection is by joining a walking club—or even starting one yourself!

Walking clubs are a wonderful way to stay consistent with exercise while building relationships. Many communities already have walking groups, so check with local parks, recreation centers, or even retired teachers associations to see if there's one near you. If you can't find one, why not create your own? Teachers are natural leaders, and starting a walking club is as simple as picking a time, a meeting spot, and spreading the word. You could invite former colleagues, neighbors, or other retirees who share your interest in staying active.

To keep things engaging, consider adding a theme to your walks. For example, you could organize "education strolls," where participants share teaching stories or discuss books they're reading. Or plan routes that explore local landmarks, nature trails, or even historical sites. Walking clubs can also double as brainstorming sessions for new projects, like volunteering opportunities or ways to mentor younger educators.

Consistency is key, so set a regular schedule—whether it's weekly or biweekly—and make it a priority. Not only will this help you stay physically sharp, but it creates a routine that keeps you socially connected and mentally engaged. What's stopping you from lacing up your sneakers and taking that first step toward a healthier, more connected retirement?

Key Takeaways:

✶ Staying mentally and physically sharp is key to a fulfilling retirement.

✶ Engage in lifelong learning, brain games, and puzzles to keep your mind sharp.

✶ Regular physical activity enhances both cognitive function and emotional well-being.

Journaling Reflections

As you navigate this vibrant chapter of your life, maintaining your mental and physical sharpness is crucial—not just for your health, but for your overall sense of fulfillment and joy. For teachers, who are lifelong learners and natural nurturers, this is a wonderful opportunity to explore new ways to stay active, engaged, and inspired. Here are some ideas to help you thrive in retirement:

1. **Start or Join a Walking Club:** Walking is a fantastic way to stay physically active while connecting with others. If you can't find a local walking club, why not start one? Invite fellow retired teachers or community members to join you for regular walks. You could even add an educational twist by exploring historical landmarks or nature trails and sharing insights along the way.

2. **Engage in Lifelong Learning:** Keep your mind sharp by taking classes or attending workshops. Many community centers, libraries, and universities offer courses on everything from creative writing to gardening. You might even consider teaching a class yourself—sharing your expertise with others can be incredibly rewarding.

3. **Volunteer in Education:** Stay connected to your passion for teaching by volunteering at local schools, tutoring students, or mentoring new educators. Your experience and wisdom are invaluable, and this is a great way to continue making a difference.

4. **Join a Book Club:** As a teacher, you've likely spent years encouraging others to read and learn. Now's the time to dive into books you've always wanted to read and discuss them with like-minded individuals. A book club can also be a wonderful way to meet new people and spark meaningful conversations.

5. **Explore Creative Hobbies:** Whether it's painting, writing, or photography, creative hobbies are excellent for mental stimulation and self-expression. Consider joining a local art group or writing circle to share your work and gain inspiration from others.

6. **Incorporate Nature Breaks:** Spending time outdoors is not only good for your physical health but for your mental well-being. Plan regular hikes, gardening sessions, or even bird-watching outings to stay connected with nature.

7. **Set a Routine for Physical Activity:** Consistency is key to staying active. Whether it's yoga, swimming, or a morning

walk, find an activity you enjoy and make it a regular part of your schedule. You could even pair it with a social element, like a fitness class or a walking buddy.

8. **Host Educational Events:** Use your teaching skills to organize workshops, seminars, or discussion groups. These events can focus on topics you're passionate about and provide a platform to connect with others who share your interests.

9. **Travel with Purpose:** Combine your love for learning and exploration by traveling to places that offer cultural or educational experiences. Join group tours or educational travel programs to meet new people and expand your horizons.

10. **Mentor Fellow Retirees:** Share your journey and insights with other retirees who may be struggling to find their footing. Your guidance could inspire them to embrace this chapter of life with confidence and enthusiasm.

What's one idea from this list that excites you the most? Let's explore how you can take the first step toward making it a reality!

1. What activities stimulate your mind and encourage you to keep learning? How can you incorporate more of these into your daily life?

_____

_____

_____

2. What are your favorite physical activities that keep you active and healthy? How can you make time for these activities regularly?

_____

_____

_____

3. What new skill or hobby have you always wanted to try but never made time for? What small steps can you take to start learning it today?

_____
_____
_____

4. When was the last time you felt mentally or physically challenged? How did you respond, and what did you learn from that experience?

_____
_____
_____

5. What routines can you create to stay mentally sharp and physically healthy as you continue to embrace this next chapter?

_____
_____
_____

STEP 7
LIVE A LIFE OF GRATITUDE

THE POWER OF BEING GRATEFUL

"When you arise in the morning, think of what a precious privilege it is to be alive." — *Marsha Linehan*

This quote celebrates the power of gratitude and appreciating each day, central to living a fulfilling refired life.

"I don't have to chase extraordinary moments to find happiness—it's right in front of me if I'm paying attention and practicing gratitude." — *Brené Brown*

This quote captures the essence of living a life of gratitude by focusing on the blessings in front of us.

Tapping into Your Gratitude

Have you experienced how tapping into gratitude for everything in your life can immediately transform your outlook for the better? If you really focus on finding things to be grateful for, the possibilities are endless. After giving thanks for the obviously positive things in your life, if you keep going, you may find yourself grateful for the simplest breath of air and the ability to walk, talk, and laugh. Everything you experience soon becomes a reason to be grateful, and suddenly, you're aware of just how blessed you truly are!

Studies show that gratitude can powerfully benefit our relationships, our work, and our physical, mental, emotional, and spiritual health. Making the sometimes awkward but completely worthwhile shift from a lack-based, negative perspective to an abundance-based, positive one has been shown to provide us with greater energy, optimism, and joy, and it helps us manage stress more easily. Plus, you can implement gratitude at any time. In fact, research shows that sustaining a gratitude practice during difficult times helps you become even more grateful than if things were going smoothly. You're less likely to take things for granted in these periods, and when circumstances have improved, your memory of the struggle helps you stay deeply grateful.

So why does gratitude make you so happy?

- **It helps you focus on the positive:** If you look at a handful of people in your life and choose to be grateful for each one, you'll find yourself naturally locating things about them that you authentically like, and the things about them you dislike quickly fade to the background.

- **It transforms the negative into positive:** Looking through the lens of gratitude, you'll see that the most harrowing challenges in your life have brought you immeasurable strength and have deepened your belief in yourself. So, they're really gifts, right?

- **It makes the big picture clearer:** Since there really is so much to be grateful for, you'll find that the minor (and even major!) stresses of life seem much more manageable. If you are continually feeling gratitude for the big positives, the negatives make much less of an impact.

- **It helps you thank those who enhance your life:** Coming into a place of continued gratitude to the universe (or whatever you perceive as your source!) helps you more easily thank others. "Thank you" is a phrase continuously on the tip of your tongue as you experience life's many gifts. As you thank others, you help them feel appreciated and, therefore, deepen your connections and the flow of love in your life. What you give, you get, so don't be surprised if more people start expressing the gratitude they feel for you to you!

Curious Where to Start Your Gratitude Practice?

As a retired teacher, you've spent your career finding the silver lining and turning challenges into opportunities for growth—so let's apply that same mindset to this new chapter of your life. Start by focusing on what's most immediate and evident. Maybe it's the joy of reconnecting with former students who share how you've impacted their lives, the pride in seeing your teaching legacy continue through others, or even the newfound freedom to explore hobbies and passions you didn't have time for before. These are the wins that deserve to be celebrated, no matter how small they may seem.

Next, dig a little deeper. What's positive but perhaps less obvious? Maybe it's the quiet satisfaction of knowing you've shaped countless lives, the personal growth you've experienced through decades of adapting to new challenges, or the enduring friendships you've built with colleagues who've become like family. These are the treasures that often go unnoticed but are so valuable.

Finally, take a closer look at the challenges you're facing in retirement. What lessons are they teaching you? How are they shaping you into a stronger, more resilient person? Perhaps adjusting to a slower pace of life has taught you to appreciate the present moment, or navigating new roles outside of teaching has pushed you to rediscover your passions. Challenges are often the greatest teachers, and as an educator, you know better than anyone how growth often comes from struggle.

By reflecting on these layers—what's immediate, what's hidden, and what's challenging—you'll not only gain a deeper appreciation for your journey but also inspire others to do the same. How can you use these reflections to mentor or connect with other retired teachers, helping them see the positives in their own lives?

And don't forget to give thanks for yourself and all you are, all you do and give, and the way you show up in the world.

Here are some tips for incorporating gratitude into your everyday life:

- **Say "thank you."** Regularly say "thank you" to the Universe, not for anything in particular, but just in general. The simple expression of these words immediately humbles you, opens your heart, and opens your eyes to all you really are thankful for!

- **Thank others, even those who've hurt you.** Thank others regularly for the things they do for you, big and small. If you remember something someone has done a while after the fact, reach out to them with thanks. They'll appreciate it so much! If there are people you don't or can't have contact with, but you still want to connect to feelings of gratitude for them, write them a note anyway—you don't have to mail it. In the note, connect with those positive and loving feelings and remember them fondly. This process can be very healing, especially if the relationship was painful. You're able to release resentments and hurt and move on with forgiveness in your heart.

- **Become the hero of your life.** As soon as you find yourself dwelling on something that's challenging or distressing, whether an individual challenge or something occurring in the world that is painful to witness, see what you can find in it to be grateful for. Reading self-help books on positive thinking and gratitude, as well as reading about the struggles that highly successful people have gone through while achieving their success, can help you see your challenges as adventures instead of punishments and yourself as the hero of your life instead of the victim. This perspective can help you see collective challenges as powerful lessons humanity is learning to become more connected and compassionate, and you'll be more motivated to contribute positively to your community because of them. Life then becomes more of an exciting journey than a daily grind.
- **Find support.** Seek out gratitude-related quotes, prayers, affirmations, and reflections that really resonate with you. They may be very simple or a little more complex. Find the ones that will stick with you through hard times and continue to lean on them for support. Perhaps there's something a wise friend or family member has told you about gratitude that continues to inspire you today. Tap into that whenever you need an extra reminder to be grateful.

Summary

Gratitude is a powerful tool for enhancing happiness and transforming your outlook on life. This chapter explored the scientifically backed benefits of gratitude and provides practical tips for incorporating it into daily life.

Key Takeaways:

✷ Gratitude shifts your focus from what's missing to what you have, creating a more positive outlook.

✷ Practicing gratitude deepens relationships and enriches your sense of fulfillment.

✷ Simple habits like keeping a gratitude journal or expressing thanks regularly can transform your retirement into a more joyful journey.

Journaling Reflections

Gratitude Walk Exercise

Take a few minutes today to appreciate nature. Go for a walk and notice only those things that are beautiful. Whether you focus on the stars above, a distant mountain range, or the tree in your backyard, try to notice the details. Give thanks for the beauty that surrounds you. Come home and write in your journal about the feelings of gratitude your walk created in you.

_____
_____
_____

The next two exercises I learned from Martin Seligman and Ronald Emmons.

Gratitude Letter/Visit Exercise

Think of someone who has contributed to your well-being whom you've never fully thanked. Write a letter to that person describing the benefits you have received. Be detailed. Describe how the actions made you feel. Take this letter and read it out loud to that person. If possible, do this in person. Take enough time to be together to exchange emotions

_____
_____
_____

Three Blessings/Gratitude Journal Exercise

Each night before bed, write at least three things that went well today. By putting your gratitude into words, you increase appreciation and memory of your blessings. If your list starts becoming repetitive, break down benefits into multiple components and reflect on each separately. Mentally label your benefits with the word "gift." When this exercise becomes habitual, it tends to increase happiness and lower depression.

_____
_____
_____

"If the only prayer you said in your whole life was, 'Thank you,' that would suffice." — *Meister Eckhart*

STEP 8
MAKE A DIFFERENCE— GIVING BACK

THE IMPORTANCE OF GIVING BACK

"Service is the rent we pay for living. It is the very purpose of life, and not something you do in your spare time."
— *Marian Wright Edelman*

This quote explains how a life of service and giving back to the community creates fulfillment.

"Service to others is the rent you pay for your room in heaven." — *Muhammad Ali*

The True Meaning of Giving Back

As you embark on your "refired" life, the profound joy of giving back can truly transform this new chapter into one of purpose and fulfillment. For teachers, who have spent their lives shaping minds and nurturing growth, this is a natural extension of your legacy. It's an opportunity to channel your energy, experience, and passion into meaningful activities that resonate with your values and leverage your unique talents.

As educators, you already know the power of connection and contribution. Research shows that acts of altruism can significantly enhance personal well-being. Dr. Stephen Post, a positive psychology expert, highlights how giving back can reduce stress, improve mental and physical health, and even extend your lifespan. Similarly, Dr. Sonja Lyubomirsky's studies reveal that generosity is closely tied to increased happiness and life satisfaction. For retired teachers, giving back not only fosters a sense of purpose but also helps combat the isolation that can sometimes accompany this stage of life, strengthening social bonds and keeping you engaged with the world.

Giving back isn't just about volunteering or making donations—it's about creating a positive impact in ways that align with your passions and strengths. As a retired teacher, you have a wealth of knowledge, skills, and experiences that can make a difference in countless ways. Here are some ideas to inspire you:

1. **Mentor the next generation of educators:** Share your expertise with new teachers by offering guidance, advice, or even classroom support. Your insights can help them navigate the challenges of the profession and grow into confident, impactful educators.

2. **Support youth programs:** Volunteer with after-school programs, literacy initiatives, or community centers.

Whether it's tutoring, leading workshops, or simply being a positive role model, your influence can shape young lives in profound ways.

3. **Advocate for education:** Use your voice to support causes that matter to you, such as equitable access to education or improved resources for schools. Join local advocacy groups or write articles to raise awareness and drive change.

4. **Engage in lifelong learning communities:** Many universities and organizations, like Osher Lifelong Learning Institutes (OLLI), offer opportunities to teach or participate in courses. Sharing your knowledge or learning alongside others can be deeply rewarding.

5. **Champion causes you care about:** Whether it's environmental sustainability, social justice, or community development, find ways to contribute to causes that align with your values. This could involve volunteering, fundraising, or even starting your own initiative.

6. **Create a legacy project:** Consider writing a book, creating a curriculum, or developing resources that reflect your expertise and passion. These contributions can continue to impact others long after you've shared them.

By giving back in ways that align with your passions, you'll not only enrich your own life but leave a lasting impact on your community and beyond. What's one cause or activity that excites you most? Let's explore how you can take the first step toward making it a reality!

Ways to Give Back

1. **Volunteer:** Use your skills and time to support local nonprofits, schools, or community centers. Volunteering allows for direct engagement with others and witnessing the impact of your contributions firsthand.

2. **Mentorship:** Impart your life lessons and professional knowledge to younger individuals. Mentoring is a gratifying way to give back, guiding others toward success.

3. **Community Engagement:** Get involved in community projects like park cleanups or local festivals. These initiatives enhance communal life and contribute to a vibrant neighborhood.

4. **Philanthropy:** Financial contributions to causes that reflect your values can make a significant difference, no matter the amount.

5. **Advocacy:** Advocate for policies and changes that benefit the community or the environment. Your voice can affect lives on a large scale.

Benefits of Giving Back

The rewards of giving back are manifold, providing happiness, fulfillment, and a robust sense of purpose. Giving back also facilitates social interactions, leading to new friendships and broader networks. Importantly, staying active through charitable work helps maintain mental sharpness and emotional resilience.

From the Cockpit to the Construction Site

David Conway's journey from an airline pilot to a humanitarian is a captivating story of profound transformation and commitment to improving the lives of others. His career started in the cockpit, soaring across the skies as a captain for US Airways, where he relished the exhilaration of flight and the unique opportunity to bridge continents and cultures. However, the demanding nature of his job often kept him away from home, making him a "part-time husband and part-time father," which weighed heavily on him over the years.

In 1994, a subtle shift began when Dave first volunteered with Habitat for Humanity. What started as a simple act of curiosity grew into a passionate mission, eventually intertwining his fate with the organization. After retiring from a brief stint in corporate flying, Dave felt increasingly drawn to the impactful work of building homes and fostering communities with Habitat for Humanity.

Dave's role within Habitat extended beyond construction; he became a leader and advocate, serving on the organization's Board of Directors, acting as a project coordinator, and eventually becoming the Chairman of the Board. His efforts reached global scales, participating in projects across Europe, the Philippines, Korea, and South Africa, and significantly contributing to building homes and spreading hope.

This transition marked a significant shift from a life of isolation high above the clouds to one deeply rooted in community and service on the ground. Dave's experiences with Habitat allowed him to confront the harsh realities of poverty and housing issues firsthand, contrasting sharply with his former life. Picking up the hammer became a symbolic gesture of his newfound vision—acknowledging and addressing the dire needs of the underprivileged.

David Conway's story transcends the physical construction of homes; it's about constructing lives, including his own. As he moved into his later years, he discovered a deeper fulfillment and a renewed sense of purpose, epitomizing the concept of "refiring" one's life. This transition into a period of vibrant contribution and spiritual growth shows that regardless of one's past roles, opportunities always exist for service and self-discovery. His path from navigating airplanes to leading building projects demonstrates a life reimagined and fully engaged with the world in a profoundly meaningful way.

David Conway's journey from an airline pilot to a humanitarian worker is a compelling tale of transformation and dedication to making a significant impact on the lives of others. His story begins in the cockpit of commercial jets and ends in the far-flung corners of the globe, where he devotes his life to humanitarian efforts.

What's Next for You? Finding Purpose Beyond the Career You Knew

David Conway's journey is a powerful reminder that our careers don't define us—our impact does. His transition from airline captain to humanitarian leader proves that there's always a new way to serve, contribute, and create meaning in our lives, no matter where we've been before.

Now, it's your turn.

✷ What cause or mission has been calling to you?

✷ How can your past skills and experiences be repurposed to help others?

✷ What steps can you take today to move toward a more fulfilling and purpose-driven next chapter?

Like Dave, you have the opportunity to build something bigger than yourself—whether through volunteering, mentoring, leadership, or hands-on service.

→ **Your next mission is waiting. How will you make a lasting impact?**

Isabel Villar: A Lifetime of Guidance, A Legacy of Empowerment

Isabel Villar's journey from a dedicated school guidance counselor to a transformative community leader is a testament to the power of purpose and the enduring impact of compassion. Her story serves as an inspiring beacon for those seeking to make a difference, proving that retirement can be a launchpad for even greater achievements.

For decades, Isabel poured her heart and soul into guiding young minds as a school guidance counselor in White Plains, New York. She was the compass that helped countless students navigate the tumultuous waters of adolescence, providing them with the support and direction they needed to chart their course through academic and personal challenges. However, Isabel's keen eye and compassionate heart couldn't ignore the struggles unfolding beyond the school walls.

In the vibrant tapestry of White Plains, Isabel saw a community in need. Hispanic immigrants, drawn by the promise of a better life, found themselves grappling with the harsh realities of their new home. Parents worked multiple jobs, stretching themselves thin to provide for their families. Children struggled to keep up in school, caught between two languages and cultures. Families faced the daunting task of navigating unfamiliar systems without the necessary resources or knowledge. For Isabel, this wasn't just a problem—it was a call to action.

With unwavering determination, Isabel embarked on a dual mission. By day, she continued her role as a guidance counselor, shaping young lives. By night, she became a community advocate, founding El Centro Hispano—an organization dedicated to supporting Hispanic families in White Plains. What began as a modest grassroots effort, offering tutoring, language assistance, and cultural support, soon blossomed into an invaluable community resource.

Retirement, for Isabel, wasn't an ending but a new beginning. It was a chance to "refire" rather than retire. Freed from the constraints of her day job, she channeled her energy and passion fully into El Centro Hispano. Under her visionary leadership, the organization flourished, expanding its services to include educational support, legal assistance, health resources, and leadership development programs. Isabel's vision was crystal clear: to empower Hispanic individuals and families, equipping them with the tools and confidence to thrive in every aspect of life.

Isabel's commitment to her community didn't stop at providing services. She understood the importance of permanence and stability. With characteristic determination, she spearheaded efforts to purchase a building, ensuring El Centro Hispano had a permanent home—a physical embodiment of the organization's enduring commitment to the community. She assembled a team of dedicated professionals and volunteers who shared her passion for service, creating a powerhouse of support and advocacy.

Isabel Villar's story is a powerful reminder that our greatest contributions often come in life's later chapters. She didn't just fill her retirement days—she filled them with purpose, passion, and profound impact. Her journey from school counselor to community pillar demonstrates that retirement isn't about stepping back, but about stepping forward into a life of even greater meaning and influence.

As we reflect on Isabel's remarkable journey, we're reminded of the immense potential that lies within each of us. Her story challenges us to look beyond conventional notions of retirement and to ask ourselves: "What legacy do I want to leave? How can I use my skills, experiences, and passions to make a lasting difference?"

Isabel's life work proves that it's never too late to start something meaningful, to tackle a pressing problem, or to be the change we wish to see in the world. She shows us that our most fulfilling chapter may still be ahead, waiting to be written. Whether it's starting a non-profit, mentoring the next generation, or advocating for a cause close to our hearts, we all have the power to create ripples of positive change that extend far beyond our immediate reach.

Let Isabel Villar's story be a catalyst for your own journey of purpose and impact. As you contemplate your next chapter, remember that your accumulated wisdom, skills, and passion are invaluable assets. The world needs your unique contributions now more than ever. So, ask yourself: "What's my El Centro Hispano? What community, cause, or dream am I ready to pour my heart into?"

Your retirement years can be more than a time of rest—they can be a time of renaissance, a period of renewed purpose and unprecedented impact. Like Isabel, you have the power to transform lives, build legacies, and leave an indelible mark on your community. The only question is: Are you ready to refire?

Remember, it's not about the years in your life, but the life in your years. Isabel Villar's story isn't just about what she did—it's about what's possible for all of us. So, take that first step. Embrace your passion. Pursue your purpose. Your greatest contribution to the world may be just beginning.

What's Next for You? Turning Passion into Lasting Impact

Isabel Villar's journey proves that retirement isn't the end—it's a new beginning filled with purpose, passion, and impact. She took the wisdom, skills, and heart she cultivated throughout her career and channeled them into a mission that transformed an entire community. Her story is a powerful reminder that our most meaningful work can come in life's later chapters.

Now, it's your turn.

★ What cause or mission ignites a fire within you?

★ How can you use your experience and talents to uplift others?

★ What bold step can you take today toward creating a legacy of impact?

Like Isabel, you have the opportunity to step forward into a life of even greater meaning—whether that means mentoring, volunteering, starting an initiative, or advocating for a cause close to your heart.

→ **Your next chapter is waiting to be written. How will you make a difference?**

A Teacher's Heart, A Leader's Vision: Carol Noble's Inspiring Journey

In the heart of Connecticut, a passionate advocate for retired teachers is making waves. Meet Carol Noble, the dynamic President of the Association of Retired Teachers of Connecticut (ARTC), whose journey from classroom to boardroom is nothing short of inspiring. After bidding farewell to the classroom, Carol didn't hang up her hat. Instead, she channeled her lifelong dedication to education into a new mission: Ensuring that those who shaped young minds could enjoy their well-deserved retirement with dignity and security.

Carol's leadership extends beyond the boardroom. Her extensive experience in politics as a legislative council member for twenty-four years, where she served as president, majority leader, and president pro tempore, has profoundly shaped her approach. She understands the importance of listening and representing the voice of the people, skills that now enhance her ability to negotiate and advocate for retired teachers.

With the same fervor she once used to inspire students, Carol now rallies for the rights of retired educators. Her days are filled with impassioned speeches, strategic planning, and relentless advocacy. "Our teachers gave their all," Carol often says. "Now it's our turn to give back to them." Her leadership style is a masterclass in communication, bridging the gap between retirees and legislators by translating complex policies into actionable plans. Carol's ability to connect with people from all walks of life has turned ARTC into a formidable force in Connecticut's political landscape.

But Carol's impact goes beyond policy changes. She's inspiring a new wave of retired teachers to stay engaged and active. "Retirement isn't the end of our journey," she reminds her colleagues. "It's a new beginning, a chance to shape the future of education from a different perspective." Carol's story is a testament to the power of purpose. Her unwavering commitment to her fellow educators serves as a beacon of hope and a call to action, proving that the passion for teaching and the desire to make a difference don't diminish with age—they evolve and grow stronger.

As Carol continues to lead ARTC into the future, she's not just securing benefits for today's retirees. She's paving the way for generations of educators to come, ensuring that the noble profession of teaching is honored and respected long after the last bell rings. Carol Noble's journey reminds us all that our potential to impact lives doesn't end with retirement. It's a powerful message to every teacher: Your voice matters, your experience is valuable, and your ability to create change is limitless. In Carol's world, retirement isn't a time to slow down—it's a time to stand up, speak out, and make a difference.

What's Next for You? Leading with Purpose Beyond Retirement

Carol Noble's journey proves that retirement isn't about stepping away—it's about stepping forward into a new chapter of leadership, advocacy, and impact. She has taken the dedication and passion she once poured into the classroom and channeled it into a mission that uplifts, protects, and empowers retired educators.

Now, it's your turn.

- ✶ What cause or community could benefit from your experience and leadership?
- ✶ How can you use your voice to advocate for meaningful change?
- ✶ What steps can you take today to remain engaged, active, and purpose-driven?

Like Carol, you have the opportunity to transform retirement into a time of action, influence, and impact—whether through advocacy, mentoring, volunteering, or leadership.

→ Your next chapter is waiting. How will you make a difference?

Karen Cassidy: Creating a Home for the Forgotten in Their Final Days

Some call it a calling. Others call it a mission. For Karen Cassidy, it was both.

As a palliative care nurse practitioner, Karen saw the harsh reality of end-of-life care—and the gaping hole in the system that left so many dying alone.

Everyone assumes hospice care ensures dignity in one's final days. But what happens if you have no home? No family to provide twenty-four-hour care? For many, that meant dying alone in shelters, on the streets, or in empty homes—left to navigate their last moments in isolation.

Karen refused to accept that fate for those in need. She knew she could do something about it.

And so, Hildegard House was born—a place where no one dies alone.

Hildegard House is not a hospital. It's not a nursing home. It's something far more profound—a home for those with nowhere else to go.

Karen and her team of sixty-five compassionate volunteers become the family these residents no longer have. They bathe, feed, comfort, and hold the hands of those in their final days, ensuring no one takes their last breath in loneliness.

Hildegard House is completely free of charge.

Unlike traditional hospice care, where patients must have financial resources or a full-time caregiver, Hildegard House never asks for money and never bills insurance companies.

Instead, they rely entirely on donations and the kindness of strangers.

Because dignity shouldn't come with a price tag.

Before founding Hildegard House in Louisville, Kentucky, Karen worked in a community hospital where she often had no choice but to discharge terminally ill patients who had nowhere to go.

She remembers the heartbreak of giving homeless patients taxi fare—not to a safe, comforting space, but to a shelter where they would die alone.

She recalls watching families struggle, unable to care for their loved ones around the clock while still balancing jobs and responsibilities.

The inequality of end-of-life care was glaring. And Karen couldn't ignore it.

"Seeing those in need and knowing I had the skills to do something about it was compelling," she says.

So she did something.

Starting Hildegard House was no small feat. But Karen was relentless.

She leaned on every skill, every experience, and every connection she had built over her lifetime.

As a former tenured professor of nursing, she had the medical knowledge to understand what was needed. With an Executive MBA, she knew how to navigate financial statements and manage operations. Having run for city council, she had the confidence to ask for funding, knock on doors, and advocate for change.

"I tell people I have been preparing for this role for all of my sixty-two years," Karen says.

With donations from local businesses, foundations, and even former residents' families, she transformed an old convent into a haven of peace and dignity.

One angelic general contractor even volunteered to renovate the entire space—a testament to the generosity that fuels Hildegard House.

Since opening, Hildegard House has cared for sixty-two individuals—each with a unique story, but all with the same need: a place to pass with dignity, surrounded by love.

There was Jim, a veteran with liver cancer who had been spending his last months crashing on friends' couches. Hildegard House gave him a home for his final six weeks, and after he passed, a veterans' organization ensured he received a proper burial fit for a hero.

Then there was Johnny, who had been cared for by his young grandchildren after losing his wife. He didn't want to be a burden, but he was also terrified of dying alone. His family stayed with him every night until visiting hours ended—until the evening he passed peacefully, knowing he was safe, loved, and not alone.

For those without family, Hildegard House becomes their family. And for those who have loved ones who simply can't provide round-the-clock care, it becomes a second home, a place of comfort, a place of peace.

The name Hildegard House isn't just symbolic—it was inspired by Hildegard of Bingen, a twelfth-century Benedictine mystic, healer, and saint.

Hildegard believed in caring for the dying, tending to the sick, and providing comfort to those in need.

Karen has carried that spirit forward into the twenty-first century—creating a place where compassion isn't just a word, but a way of life.

If Karen could leave the world with one message, it's this:

"Follow your dreams. Don't say you can't do it. Be flexible. And most importantly, believe in miracles. They can come true."

Hildegard House shouldn't exist—not in a world where hospice care is often a privilege, not a right. And yet, it does.

Because one woman refused to accept the unacceptable.

Because generosity is more powerful than scarcity.

Because love, dignity, and compassion belong to everyone—especially in their final moments.

What's Next for You?

Karen's story is a reminder that one person can create profound change—not just in how people live, but in how they leave this world.

✶ Where do you see a need in your community?

✶ How can you use your skills, time, or resources to make a difference?

✶ What small step can you take today that could lead to something bigger than yourself?

Like Karen, you have the power to change lives—and maybe even work miracles.

→ **Take the first step. Someone is waiting for you.**

Living My Life as a Thank You

Gratitude isn't just something I practice—it's a way of life. My favorite words, "I live my life as a thank you," are a reflection of how deeply gratitude has shaped my journey. It's not just about saying thank you; it's about experiencing life with a grateful heart, embracing each moment as a gift.

The first thing I do each morning, before the day fully begins, is sit in my quiet spot and write down five things I am grateful for. This simple habit started years ago after watching an Oprah show about gratitude, and it has been life-changing. Taking just a few moments to acknowledge the blessings in my life, no matter how big or small, sets the tone for my entire day.

I also walk in nature as an act of gratitude—taking in the beauty of the sunrise and sunset, feeling the change of seasons, and appreciating the simple fact that I can witness these wonders. Just being present with nature reminds me that every day is a gift, and I am fortunate to experience it.

Living with gratitude has made me a more positive and joyful person. Science supports what I've experienced firsthand—gratitude rewires the brain, boosts happiness, and creates a greater sense of well-being. Even in difficult times, when I pause and give thanks, I feel renewed and resilient. I am happier because I choose to see the abundance around me rather than focus on what's missing.

One of my greatest joys is knowing I am alive to see my children grow into amazing adults and spend time with my grandchildren. Each day, I recognize how precious this life is. My gratitude journal has become a cherished tool, reminding me daily of the blessings that surround me.

What's Next for You?

My story is a reminder that gratitude isn't just a feeling—it's a way of living that can transform your perspective, your happiness, and your future.

- ✶ How can you bring more gratitude into your daily life?
- ✶ What simple practice—like journaling, walking in nature, or pausing to give thanks—can help you see life's abundance?
- ✶ How will choosing gratitude today shape the way you experience tomorrow?

Like me, you have the power to shift your mindset, embrace joy, and create a life filled with appreciation and purpose.

→ Take the first step. A more fulfilling, gratitude-filled life is waiting for you.

Journaling Reflections

Writing down your thoughts allows you to reflect on your experiences, clarify your goals, and stay motivated as you find meaningful ways to contribute. Start by asking yourself questions like: What causes or communities resonate most with me? How can I use my unique skills as an educator to make an impact? What small steps can I take today to begin giving back?

Here are five journaling exercises to help you explore and deepen your commitment to giving back:

1. Gratitude for Help Received:

- **Exercise:** Write about a time someone helped you in a significant way. Describe the situation in detail, how it made you feel, and the difference it made in your life. Reflect on how you can pay this kindness forward to others.

_____

_____

_____

- **Purpose:** This exercise helps cultivate gratitude and inspires thoughts on how to extend kindness to others, fostering a cycle of generosity.

2. Visualizing Your Positive Impact:

- **Exercise:** Imagine it's five years from now, and you've been consistently giving back to your community or a cause you care about. Describe in your journal what you have done, the challenges you faced, and the outcomes of your efforts. How has your contribution made a difference?

_____
_____
_____

- **Purpose:** This exercise helps you visualize potential long-term commitments and their benefits, providing motivation and clarifying your aspirations in giving back.

3. Acts of Kindness Log:

- **Exercise:** Keep a weekly log of small acts of kindness you perform. These can be as simple as smiling at a stranger, holding a door open, or helping a neighbor. At the end of the week, review your actions and reflect on how they made you feel and possibly affected others.

_____
_____
_____

- **Purpose:** This exercise encourages regular acts of kindness, reinforcing the habit and highlighting the positive emotions associated with altruistic behaviors.

4. Identifying Causes:

- **Exercise:** Write a list of issues or causes that resonate deeply with you. For each, jot down why it matters to you and how you might contribute your time, resources, or skills. Research organizations that align with these causes and note how you could get involved.

_____
_____
_____

- **Purpose:** This exercise helps pinpoint your passions and potential areas for contribution, making your giving back more focused and meaningful.

5. *Letter to the Future Self:*

- **Exercise:** Write a letter to your future self, describing the kind of philanthropic work you hope to have achieved. Detail the values you want to live by and the kinds of contributions you hope to make.

_____

_____

_____

- **Purpose:** This exercise serves as a motivational letter and a personal reminder of your philanthropic goals, helping you stay committed to and focused on giving back.

These journaling exercises not only serve as personal reflections but as actionable steps toward a more giving and fulfilling life. Beyond journaling, connecting with others who share your passion for enriching their communities can amplify your efforts. Joining groups—whether they're retired teachers associations, local volunteer organizations, or even online communities—provides a supportive space to exchange ideas, share experiences, and inspire one another. For example, you might join a group focused on mentoring young educators or supporting literacy programs. These connections not only spark new ideas but also remind you that you're not alone in your journey.

Conclusion

Putting It All Together

As I've been mentioning throughout this book, all of these pieces fit inextricably together. Having a sense of purpose and realizing your strengths fuels your desire to engage in activities that reflect both.

Those activities can be prioritized and organized into your schedule, and that schedule can be further used to manifest your largest goals and aspirations. These, in turn, will be tackled with the most gusto if you are healthy and mentally sharp.

Without the knowledge that you have a purpose, you may languish. You may find yourself shutting yourself indoors, watching television, and trying to hide from yourself and others.

I once heard the story of a retired man who received a phone call one day. He discovered that, because he had been such a good customer at the video store, he had won a gift certificate to rent movies for free. This little jolt was, in fact, the catalyst that made him realize he was spending all his time inside watching videos. At that point, he decided he needed to change his life.

Dealing with Loss

While retirement can be the most wonderful time of life, it is also the phase of our lives when perhaps we will face more loss than any other time. We may be mourning the loss of loved ones, or regretting choices we've made in the past that have led us to this point. Risks of trying to avoid the pain associated with loss seem to increase. Risk factors include turning to narcotic substances to ease the pain or boredom we may feel.

Behaviors involving alcohol and drug abuse are similar to those involving staying indoors watching television or movies. Both behaviors stem from boredom, from not knowing what else to do. Alcohol and all kinds of drug abuse happen even with older people, not just with young people specifically, because people feel a lack of meaning and purpose in their lives.

These behaviors happen when people have disconnected from their work. They happen when they don't know what their mission is. They happen when they don't know what their strengths are. And they happen when they have no purpose.

A particular danger exists for former big executives who were extremely important in their jobs. Once retired, they may feel useless. I remember the story of George Eastman, the man who founded Kodak. After he "retired," he killed himself. He left behind a note that said, "My work is done. Why wait?"

People who directly face and handle the losses and sadness they feel are in a much better position to move on and rise up from the ashes. Maintaining relationships, finding outside interests, and applying the general methods we've been highlighting for taking charge of yourself and your life are all tried and true ways to prevent being crippled by loss and regret. There's still time to change the road you're on.

Not the End—A New Beginning!

The Refire mission is about reigniting your passion and embracing each day with purpose and possibility. As an educator, you've spent years inspiring others—now it's time to turn that inspiration inward. By taking intentional steps, you're choosing a life filled with joy, fulfillment, and deep satisfaction beyond the classroom.

You don't have to settle for stagnation or feel adrift in this new chapter. Instead, one step at a time, with patience and self-compassion, you'll uncover the vibrant, radiant individual who's been waiting to shine. This is your moment to create, explore, and thrive on your own terms.

Refire now. As a fellow educator, I've made it my mission to share this message with teachers everywhere. I hope it inspires you to dream bigger, reach further, and discover a life beyond teaching that's even more rewarding than you imagined.

Questions to Ponder

By reflecting on these questions and taking action, you can ensure that your retirement is not only enjoyable but also rich with personal growth and satisfaction.

How will you refire your life in your next chapter? Consider what refiring means to you in the context of your retirement. It could involve redefining your purpose, embracing new challenges, or continuing to grow through new learning opportunities. Think about the activities and goals that will make you leap out of bed each morning with excitement. Whether it's committing to a fitness regimen, volunteering in areas you are passionate about, or even starting a part-time business, identify specific actions that align with your vision of a vibrant, engaging retirement. Reflect on how these activities contribute to your sense of fulfillment and excitement about the future, ensuring that each day of your retirement is as enriching and purposeful as the last.

What are the passions and interests you have not yet explored that you could pursue in retirement? Consider the hobbies or activities you've always been curious about but never had time to explore. Retirement offers the perfect opportunity to delve into these interests. Whether it's learning a new language, taking up gardening, or exploring photography, think about what excites you and how you can incorporate these activities into your daily life.

How do your values align with your current retirement plans, and what changes might you consider to better align them? Reflect on your core values and examine how well they align with your current retirement plans. Are you living in a way that reflects your beliefs and priorities? If discrepancies exist, identify changes you can make to ensure your lifestyle is a true reflection of your values.

What are the biggest fears you have about retirement, and how can you address them to move forward with confidence? Identify any fears or anxieties you have about retirement, such as the fear of isolation or financial insecurity. Acknowledging these fears is the first step toward addressing them. Consider seeking advice from financial advisors or counselors to develop strategies to mitigate these concerns.

How can you use your skills and experiences to contribute to your community or help others in this stage of your life? Think about how you can use your professional skills or personal talents to contribute to your community. It could be through mentoring young professionals, volunteering at local organizations, or offering free classes in your area of expertise.

What does a fulfilling day look like to you now, and how does that compare to your pre-retirement life? Imagine your ideal day in retirement. What activities does it include? Who are you spending time with? What are you most looking forward to? Use these reflections to start shaping your days to be as fulfilling as possible.

How can you maintain and build new connections that enrich your life and keep you engaged? Evaluate your current social connections and consider how you can strengthen them. Perhaps schedule regular meet-ups with friends, join a club or group that shares your interests, or use technology to stay in touch with distant family members.

What are the most important goals you want to achieve in the next five years, and what steps can you take now to start achieving them? Write down three to five major goals you want to achieve in the next five years. These could relate to personal development, travel, health, or family. Outline the first few steps needed to pursue each goal, and consider setting timelines to track your progress.

How can you ensure your retirement is both physically and mentally active? Plan how you will keep both your mind and body active. It might involve regular physical exercise, such as yoga or swimming, coupled with mental exercises like puzzles, reading, or learning a new skill or subject.

In what ways can you continue to challenge yourself and grow intellectually in retirement? Identify ways to challenge yourself intellectually. It could be through taking courses at a local college, joining a book club, or engaging in lively discussions with peers. Setting educational goals can provide a sense of accomplishment and continuous growth.

How will you mark the transition into retirement with a celebration that reflects your new beginning? Think about marking the start of your retirement with a celebration that symbolizes your transition into this new phase of life. This could be a small gathering with close family and friends where you share your plans and dreams for the future, or a larger event with a theme that reflects your retirement aspirations.

What new skills or hobbies are you interested in developing during retirement? Consider the range of interests you might not have had time to explore while working. Whether it's a craft, a sport, a language, or a field of study, think about what intrigues you and how you might go about learning it. Plan how you can integrate these new skills into your daily routine to keep your mind and body engaged and continually growing.

How do you plan to maintain and enhance your health and wellness during retirement? Health is a crucial aspect that significantly affects your quality of life in retirement. Reflect on your current health practices and how you might improve or adjust them. Consider setting goals related to nutrition, exercise, mental health, and preventative care. Think about the support systems and resources you might need, such as joining a health club, participating in wellness programs, or even collaborating with healthcare professionals to keep your health on track for a long and active retirement.

Thought-Provoking Quotes

These quotes are meant to inspire, empower, and challenge you to be better than you've ever been.

"You must take personal responsibility. You cannot change the circumstances, the seasons, or the wind but you can change yourself."
— *Jim Rohn*

"Our deepest fear is not that we are inadequate. Our deepest fear is that we are powerful beyond measure. It is our Light, not our Darkness, that most frightens us."
— *Marianne Williamson*

"Ninety-nine percent of all failures come from people who have a habit of making excuses."
— *George Washington Carver*

"Life is like a combination lock: your job is to find the right numbers, in the right order so you can have anything you want."
— *Brian Tracy*

"If we did all the things we are capable of doing, we would literally astound ourselves."

— *Thomas Edison*

"People who use their strengths more are happier, more confident, have higher levels of energy, are more resilient and are more likely to achieve their goals. Many people die with their music still in them."

— *Oliver Wendell Holmes*

"If I'd known I was going to live so long, I'd have taken better care of myself."

— *Leon Eldrige*

A Splendid Torch

"This is the true joy in life, the being used for a purpose recognized by yourself as a mighty one; the being a force of nature instead of a feverish, selfish little clod of ailments and grievances complaining that the world will not devote itself to making you happy.

"I am of the opinion that my life belongs to the whole community, and as long as I live it is my privilege to do whatever I can.

"I want to be thoroughly used up when I die, for the harder I work the more I live. I rejoice in life for its own sake. Life is no 'brief candle' for me. It is a sort of splendid torch which I have got hold of for the moment, and I want to make it burn as brightly as possible before handing it on to future generations."

— *George Bernard Shaw*

From Inspiration to Action: Your Refire Journey Awaits!

Choose your next step to keep the momentum alive:

1. **The 30-Day Refire Challenge** – A guided plan to spark purpose, build momentum, and create meaningful progress in just one month.
2. **The Refire Study Group** – A collaborative space to connect, share insights, and dive deeper into strategies for thriving in retirement.

30-Day Refire Challenge

I know I've thrown a lot of information, exercises, and hope-filled inspiration at you in these pages. But to make this truly transformational, you need to do two things: first, admit that you are ready to step boldly into your next chapter with purpose, and second, commit to taking consistent action. To help you do just that, I've organized everything we've covered in this book into a 30-day challenge designed to get you moving, keep you on track, and show you exactly where you are in the process. All the information you need to complete the challenge is already in your hands, but if you're looking for extra support and inspiration, I invite you to join the Sip and Chat monthly meeting. It's a space where like-minded educators connect, share tips, and cheer each other on. We'll be waiting to greet you and celebrate your progress, so come join us! Visit https://www.refiredontretire.com/sip-chat/ to sign up. Let's do this together!

Week 1: Shift Gears

This week is all about embracing the transition from the classroom to retirement. Start by reflecting on what excites you about this new chapter and what feels uncertain. For example, write about how you'll fill the time you once spent grading papers or planning lessons. Create a vision board with images of hobbies, travel, or family time to visualize your ideal retirement.

Week 2: Find Your Purpose

Rediscover what lights you up! Reflect on passions you may have set aside during your teaching career. Maybe you've always wanted to write a children's book or volunteer at a literacy program. Research opportunities to engage with these interests and take one small step, like signing up for a local workshop or reaching out to an organization.

Week 3: Discover and Live from Your Strengths

Tap into the skills that made you a great teacher. Were you known for your creativity in lesson planning or your ability to inspire students? Write down your top strengths and brainstorm how to use them in retirement. For instance, if you excelled at mentoring, consider becoming a mentor for new teachers or leading a community group.

Week 4: Manage Time, Stay Connected, and Stay Sharp

Create a balanced daily schedule that includes physical activity, mental stimulation, and social connection. Join a walking club for retired teachers or start a book club to stay connected with peers. Try something new, like learning a language or taking up yoga, to keep your mind and body sharp.

Final Days: Gratitude and Giving Back

End the challenge by focusing on gratitude and making a difference. Start a gratitude journal, listing three things you're thankful for each day. Then, find a way to give back—volunteer to tutor students, donate books to a school, or organize a fundraiser for education.

You've taken the first step toward embracing a refired life—a life filled with meaning,

fulfillment, and purpose. This 30-day challenge is more than just a series of tasks, it's a jumpstart to rediscovering your passions, reigniting your strengths, and creating a life that excites and inspires you every single day. Retirement isn't the end of your story—it's the beginning of a bold new chapter where you can live intentionally, connect deeply, and make a lasting impact. And remember, you don't have to do this alone! Sign up for the Sip and Chat monthly meeting to connect with other like-minded educators, sharing tips, inspiration, and camaraderie. Together, we'll ignite your next adventure and make this the most rewarding chapter of your life yet! https://www.refiredontretire.com/sip-chat/

The Refire Study Group

Retirement is a fresh start for teachers—a chance to rediscover purpose and joy beyond the classroom. After years of shaping young minds, it's natural to seek clarity and connection in this new chapter.

The Refire Study Group creates a safe, uplifting space to connect with fellow educators who share your journey. Through meaningful conversations, shared reflections, and actionable steps, you'll gain fresh perspectives, build lasting friendships, and stay inspired to embrace this exciting phase of life.

Whether you're reigniting old passions, exploring new opportunities, or simply finding joy in the everyday, this group is here to guide and support you. To help you get started, I've created the Refire Study Group Starter Kit—a resource to empower you to form your own community of like-minded educators. Together, you'll explore the lessons of Refire: A Roadmap for Teachers to Rediscover Purpose and Joy in Retirement, share insights, and support one another as you thrive in this transformative journey."

The best part? You don't need me to guide you—this kit provides everything you need to get started and keep your group thriving. Whether you're meeting in person or virtually, the Study Group Kit makes it easy to build meaningful connections and create a space for encouragement, accountability, and inspiration.

What's Inside the Study Group Kit?

1. **Study Group Checklist:** A step-by-step guide to help you organize your group, set goals, and establish a schedule that works for everyone.
2. **Sample Agenda Template:** A ready-to-use structure for your meetings, including time for check-ins, discussions, and actionable takeaways.
3. **Discussion Questions:** Thought-provoking prompts tailored to the book's themes, designed to spark meaningful conversations and deeper reflection.
4. **Printable Worksheets:** Tools to help you and your group members set goals, track progress, and reflect on key insights.
5. **Tips for Success:** Practical advice for keeping your group engaged, focused, and supportive.

Why Include This Kit?

I believe that connection is key to rediscovering purpose and joy. By forming a study group, you'll not only deepen your understanding of the book's lessons but also create a supportive community that inspires and uplifts. This kit is my way of making it easier for you to take that step.

Download Your Study Group Kit Today!

Visit www.refiredontretire.com/study-group to download your free Refire Study Group Kit and start building your community today. Together, you can reignite your passions and embrace this next chapter with purpose and joy!

Appendix
Essential Reads to Fuel Your Refire Journey

As you embark on your journey to refire your life, it's essential to have resources that inspire, guide, and motivate you. The following curated list of 40 inspiring books offers powerful insights from a wide range of voices—exploring topics like purpose, creativity, resilience, and aging with grace. Whether you're seeking practical advice for reinventing yourself or looking for stories of transformation, these books provide the tools and inspiration to help you navigate the next chapter of your life with joy, fulfillment, and purpose.

These forty inspiring books serve as a wellspring of wisdom, encouragement, and practical guidance for anyone looking to refire their life. Each book offers unique insights into embracing change, discovering new purpose, and navigating the challenges and opportunities that come with aging. Whether you're seeking to reignite passions, strengthen connections, or cultivate a life of meaning and fulfillment, these resources are here to support you every step of the way. Remember, your next chapter can be as vibrant and purposeful as you choose—these books will help you make it a reality.

I want to thank all the wonderful authors and teachers who have been my role models. They inspired, encouraged, and motivated me to take charge of my new liberty, and to use it as an indispensable time to refire, recharge, and revive myself as I entered this new chapter in my life. Their message has been loud and clear, so I decided when I "retired" from my position as an assistant high school principal that "refiring" was my only option, and I am glad I did. I live a highly "refired" life and am on a mission to help anyone I come in contact with to think of "refiring" and reimagining their next chapter.

A special thank you to my friends and family for their unfailing encouragement and support on my refired journey.

1. **Aging as a Spiritual Practice: A Contemplative Guide to Growing Older and Wiser** by Lewis Richmond
   A guide to embracing aging as a spiritual journey, filled with wisdom on finding peace and purpose in later years.

2. **Aging Well: Surprising Guideposts to a Happier Life from the Landmark Harvard Study of Adult Development** by George E. Vaillant
   Based on a long-term Harvard study, this book provides practical insights on living a healthier, more fulfilling life in later years.

3. **Being Mortal: Medicine and What Matters in the End** by Atul Gawande
   A powerful exploration of how to live meaningfully as we age and retain autonomy and purpose in life's final stages.

4. **Big Magic: Creative Living Beyond Fear** by Elizabeth Gilbert
   Encourages readers to embrace creativity and pursue their passions fearlessly, regardless of age or stage in life.

5. **Breaking the Age Code: How Your Beliefs About Aging Determine How Long and Well You Live** by Becca Levy
   This book challenges conventional notions about aging and reveals how our mindset influences the aging process.

6. **Designing Your Life: How to Build a Well-Lived, Joyful Life** by Bill Burnett and Dave Evans
   A practical guide to creating a fulfilling life at any stage, helping readers to approach their later years with creativity and intention.

7. **Dying to Be Me: My Journey from Cancer, to Near Death, to True Healing** by Anita Moorjani
   An inspirational story of self-discovery, healing, and living authentically, highlighting how life can change after overcoming major challenges.

8. **Falling Upward: A Spirituality for the Two Halves of Life** by Richard Rohr
   Explores how the second half of life offers new opportunities for deeper meaning and spiritual growth.

9. **Finding Meaning in the Second Half of Life: How to Finally, Really Grow Up** by James Hollis
   A guide to navigating the midlife transition and discovering deeper purpose and meaning in the later stages of life.

10. **Finding Your Own North Star: Claiming the Life You Were Meant to Live** by Martha Beck
    Beck offers a roadmap for reconnecting with your true purpose, helping readers navigate transitions and pursue a meaningful path.

11. **Grit: The Power of Passion and Perseverance** by Angela Duckworth
    This book teaches the value of resilience, persistence, and pursuing long-term goals, all essential to reinventing oneself in retirement.

12. **How to Age Joyfully: Eight Steps to a Happier, Fuller Life** by Maggy Pigott
    Practical advice on aging gracefully and joyfully, helping readers live with intention, meaning, and happiness in their later years.

13. **How to Retire Happy, Wild, and Free: Retirement Wisdom That You Won't Get from Your Financial Advisor** by Ernie J. Zelinski
    A guide to making the most of retirement by focusing on non-financial aspects such as well-being, leisure, and purpose.

14. **Life Reimagined: The Science, Art, and Opportunity of Midlife** by Barbara Bradley Hagerty
A thoughtful examination of midlife, offering tools and insights for reinventing oneself and finding new meaning in the second half of life.

15. **Man's Search for Meaning** by Viktor E. Frankl
A timeless classic that explores finding purpose and meaning in even the most challenging circumstances, offering profound insights on living with intention and gratitude.

16. **Mindfulness for Beginners: Reclaiming the Present Moment—and Your Life** by Jon Kabat-Zinn
A simple, accessible guide to practicing mindfulness, helping readers find peace and clarity as they age.

17. **My Time: Making the Most of the Rest of Your Life** by Abigail Trafford
Trafford offers insights on how to navigate the post-retirement years and create a life full of purpose and joy.

18. **Never Too Late: Your Roadmap to Reinvention (without Getting Lost Along the Way)** by Claire Cook
This book encourages readers to reinvent themselves at any age, with practical advice for embracing change and new opportunities.

19. **Option B: Facing Adversity, Building Resilience, and Finding Joy** by Sheryl Sandberg and Adam Grant
A powerful book about resilience and finding strength after loss, offering practical advice on how to move forward and live fully.

20. **Radical Acceptance: Embracing Your Life With the Heart of a Buddha** by Tara Brach
This book offers guidance on self-acceptance and mindfulness, helping readers find inner peace and purpose as they navigate life's challenges.

21. **Repacking Your Bags: Lighten Your Load for the Rest of Your Life** by Richard J. Leider and David A. Shapiro
A resource for people seeking to refire their lives by simplifying and focusing on what truly brings them joy and purpose.

22. **Retirement Reinvention: Make Your Next Act Your Best Act** by Robin Ryan
Ryan's book offers guidance on how to reimagine and reinvent your life after retirement, providing tools to craft a more fulfilling future.

23. **Second Spring: A Love Letter to Menopause** by Kate Codrington
Codrington offers a fresh, inspiring perspective on aging and embracing the menopause journey as a time of personal transformation.

24. **The Artist's Way: A Spiritual Path to Higher Creativity** by Julia Cameron
A classic guide to reigniting creativity, no matter your age, this book provides exercises and reflections to help you rediscover your artistic spirit.

25. **The Blue Zones: 9 Lessons for Living Longer from the People Who've Lived the Longest** by Dan Buettner
This book reveals the secrets of the world's healthiest, longest-lived communities and offers practical advice for living a long and fulfilled life.

26. **The Encore Career Handbook: How to Make a Living and a Difference in the Second Half of Life** by Marci Alboher
A practical guide for those looking to combine purpose and passion in their second career, offering inspiration for making a meaningful transition.

27. **The Gift of Years: Growing Older Gracefully**
by Joan Chittister
A celebration of the aging process, this book provides insights on finding joy and purpose in later life.

28. **The Happiness Curve: Why Life Gets Better After 50**
by Jonathan Rauch
Rauch explores why happiness often increases in later life, offering insights into the science and personal experiences behind this upward curve.

29. **The Longevity Economy: Unlocking the World's Fastest-Growing, Most Misunderstood Market** by Joseph F. Coughlin
This book explores how the aging population is reshaping society and the economy, offering a fresh perspective on aging as a time of opportunity.

30. **The Power of Now: A Guide to Spiritual Enlightenment**
by Eckhart Tolle
A powerful guide to living fully in the present moment, helping readers to find peace and purpose in their current stage of life.

31. **The Retirement Boom: An All-Inclusive Guide to Money, Life, and Health in Your Next Chapter** by Catherine Allen, Nancy Bearg, Rita Foley, and Jaye Smith
A comprehensive guide to planning for and thriving in retirement, covering financial, emotional, and health-related aspects of this life stage.

32. **The Second Mountain: The Quest for a Moral Life**
by David Brooks
Brooks examines how living for others, rather than self-centered pursuits, can lead to greater happiness and fulfillment in life's later chapters.

33. **The Third Chapter: Passion, Risk, and Adventure in the 25 Years After 50** by Sara Lawrence-Lightfoot
An exploration of the possibilities for growth, learning, and adventure in the "third chapter" of life, offering examples of those who have reinvented themselves after fifty.

34. **The Wisdom of Sundays: Life-Changing Insights from Super Soul Conversations** by Oprah Winfrey
A collection of spiritual teachings and life lessons from thought leaders and visionaries, offering inspiration for living with purpose and clarity.

35. **This Chair Rocks: A Manifesto Against Ageism** by Ashton Applewhite
A bold exploration of ageism and a call to embrace aging as a time of empowerment and opportunity.

36. **Thrive: The Third Metric to Redefining Success and Creating a Life of Well-Being, Wisdom, and Wonder** by Arianna Huffington
This book explores how to redefine success beyond money and power, focusing on well-being, wisdom, and giving back as keys to living a fulfilled life.

37. **What Are You Doing with the Rest of Your Life?** by Paula Payne Hardin
This book offers insight and encouragement for finding meaning, purpose, and joy in the second half of life.

38. **What Should I Do with the Rest of My Life? True Stories of Finding Success, Passion, and New Meaning in the Second Half of Life** by Bruce Frankel
Frankel shares inspiring stories of people who discovered new purpose and achieved great things later in life.

39. **When Breath Becomes Air** by Paul Kalanithi
A profound memoir on living a life of meaning, even when faced with life's most difficult challenges.

40. Your Life Calling: Reimagining the Rest of Your Life
by Jane Pauley
Jane Pauley shares stories of people who have reinvented their lives after fifty, offering inspiration for those looking to refire their life in meaningful ways.

These 40 inspiring books serve as a wellspring of wisdom, encouragement, and practical guidance for anyone looking to refire their life. Each book offers unique insights into embracing change, discovering new purpose, and navigating the challenges and opportunities that come with aging. Whether you're seeking to reignite passions, strengthen connections, or cultivate a life of meaning and fulfillment, these resources are here to support you every step of the way. Remember, your next chapter can be as vibrant and purposeful as you choose—these books will help you make it a reality.

Acknowledgements

To my mother, whose life was a shining example of courage, creativity, and resilience. I learned from her to see challenges as opportunities and to face them with determination.
She wasn't able to send money from America to buy new uniforms, so I took matters into my own hands. At just 12 years old, I turned our worn school uniforms inside out, inspired by her resourcefulness, so we could step into the new school year with confidence. That small act became a lifelong lesson in problem-solving and perseverance, shaping the way I approach challenges to this day.

Her bravery in leaving everything behind to seek a better life in America for her children is the foundation of my strength and success. She showed me that we are always meant for more—that life's challenges are stepping stones to greater purpose. I thank her for teaching me what it means to live with love, courage, and unwavering purpose.

To my daughters and grandchildren, who fill my life with joy and inspiration. Your brilliance, creativity, and unwavering support remind me every day of the beauty in this world. You are my greatest motivation and my constant source of strength.

To my husband, Harry, my steadfast supporter and biggest cheerleader. Your belief in me has been a constant source of encouragement. Thank you for standing by me through every step of this journey.

Acknowledgements

To my colleagues, whose stories and journeys are woven into the fabric of this book. To those who faced the uncertainty of leaving the classroom and found a new purpose, and to those who embraced their next chapter with passion and determination—you are my inspiration.

And to my supervisors, who encouraged my creativity and pushed me to grow, thank you for believing in me and helping me reach new heights.

To my editor, whose patience and dedication made my words shine and come alive. Your thoughtful guidance and skillful touch brought clarity and life to my writing. Thank you for helping me find my voice and ensuring that my message resonates with readers.

And finally, to myself. That 12-year-old girl who turned uniforms inside out taught me that even in the face of adversity, there's always a way forward. This book is a celebration of that spirit—a tribute to resilience, creativity, and the courage to embrace new beginnings.

About the Author

Dr. Cynthia Barnett is a passionate trailblazer whose journey from educator to visionary entrepreneur shows that life after the classroom can be even more impactful. After dedicating more than thirty years to empowering students and shaping minds, she now inspires teachers to reflect, reimagine, and reignite their purpose in bold new ways.

Driven by a desire to empower and uplift, Dr. Barnett founded Amazing Girls Science, a groundbreaking initiative designed to close the gender gap in STEAM (Science, Technology, Engineering, Arts, and Mathematics). What began as a concern over alarming statistics—like only 14 percent of computer science undergraduates being women—quickly became a mission to change the narrative for girls across the country. Through science conferences, robotics programs, and summer camps, Amazing Girls Science ignites curiosity, builds confidence, and encourages girls from elementary to high school to dream big and break barriers.

But Dr. Barnett's impact doesn't stop there. She is the heart behind the powerful movement, "Refire, Don't Retire," a philosophy that inspires educators—especially those nearing retirement—to view this season not as an end, but as a launchpad. Her mission is bold: to help one million educators reinvent their next chapter with purpose, passion, and renewed joy. She understands the deep identity shift that often comes with leaving the classroom, and she's made it her life's work to show fellow educators how to transform their teaching skills into new, meaningful ventures.

Featured in Time magazine for her work, Dr. Barnett is living proof that educators have what it takes to lead, innovate, and thrive outside of traditional roles. Her story offers a roadmap for teachers at a crossroads:

1. Your teaching expertise is powerful—and it's transferable.
2. You can still change lives, just in new and exciting ways.
3. Retirement is not the finish line—it's your invitation to reimagine, reignite, and refire.
4. Your second act can be your most impactful yet.

Through her dynamic programs, inspirational coaching, and infectious enthusiasm, Dr. Cynthia Barnett is helping a generation of teachers step boldly into what's next—creating lives filled with purpose, freedom, and fulfillment.

START LIVING YOUR REFIRED LIFE TODAY!

I hope you've enjoyed reading this book and gained valuable insights during our time together! But don't stop here—keep the momentum going. Your journey to rediscovering purpose and joy in retirement is just beginning, and I'm here to support you every step of the way. Visit refiredontretire.com to explore my programs designed to help you embrace this exciting new chapter with confidence, clarity, and enthusiasm.

And remember, you don't have to do this alone! I invite you to join me at my Sip and Chat monthly gatherings. These sessions are a wonderful opportunity to connect with like-minded educators, share your challenges, celebrate your wins, and gain inspiration for your next steps. It's a supportive and uplifting space where we cheer each other on and grow together. You'll leave each session feeling motivated and empowered to take consistent action toward your goals.

So, let's keep the conversation going! Visit www.refiredontretire.com/sip-chat to sign up and join this incredible community of educators who are embracing their next chapter with purpose and passion. I can't wait to see where this journey takes you!

To your bold and exciting next chapter,
Cynthia Barnett

Programs to Help You Elevate and Embrace Your Refired Life

Unlock the limitless possibilities of your next chapter with transformative programs designed to ignite your passion, boost your confidence, and bring your dreams to life. Each program is crafted to empower you to step fully into a vibrant, purposeful future—taking your refired life to extraordinary new heights!

The VIP Retreat Day: Your Exclusive Opportunity to Fast-Track Your Next Chapter

Imagine spending an entire day—or even a half day—devoted entirely to you, your dreams, and your future. Whether virtually or in person, The VIP Retreat Day is a unique and immersive experience designed to help you create fast results and move forward quickly in the areas of your life that need the most focus and support.

During this private, customized day, you'll receive expert coaching, personalized guidance, and powerful strategies to unlock clarity, passion, and purpose in your next chapter. We will dive deeply into what's holding you back, break through the barriers, and create a clear action plan that will transform your vision into reality.

By the end of our VIP day together, you will:

✶ Gain unshakable clarity about your goals and the direction of your new life.

✶ Feel reenergized and empowered with the confidence to take bold steps toward your dreams.

✶ Have a focused action plan tailored to your unique needs and desires so you can move forward with purpose and intention.

✶ Leave with the tools and mindset to turn your aspirations into tangible results—faster than you ever thought possible.

This day is all about you and your journey. If you're ready to make rapid progress, I invite you to schedule a complimentary call to see if The VIP Retreat Day is the right fit for you. Let's discover together how this personalized, high-impact experience can help you fast-track your success and step into a life full of possibilities!

www.refiredontretire.com/vip

Elevate and Ignite: Seminars to Empower Your Refired Journey

Dr. Barnett's Speeches and Seminars are more than just events—they are transformational experiences that take participants on an inspiring journey to design, define, and step into a crystal-clear vision of their Refired Life. Through engaging, content-rich, and interactive sessions, participants are guided to reimagine their next chapter with clarity, confidence, and purpose.

What You Will Leave With:

- ✶ A Clear Vision: You will walk away with a crystal-clear vision of the life you are reimagining. Through guided exercises, you'll gain clarity about what you truly want in this next chapter and how to make it a reality.

- ✶ Actionable Strategies: You will develop concrete steps and strategies to start living the life you've envisioned. This isn't just about dreaming—it's about creating a roadmap for real transformation.

- ✶ Inspiration and Motivation: Dr. Barnett's dynamic approach will leave you feeling energized and empowered, ready to take bold action toward your goals.

- ✶ A Reignited Sense of Purpose: You will reconnect with your passions and discover new opportunities to live a life filled with meaning, joy, and fulfillment.

Each seminar is designed to give you the tools not only to reimagine your life but to step into it, creating the future you deserve with a renewed sense of possibility.

Sip & Chat with Cynthia – A Special Gathering for Retired Educators

Join us for "Sip & Chat with Cynthia," a warm and welcoming monthly Zoom gathering designed exclusively for retired educators. Held on the first Monday of every month from 5:00–6:00 PM EST, this is your opportunity to connect with like-minded former teachers, share experiences, and find inspiration for your next chapter.

In this uplifting and supportive space, we'll explore topics like rediscovering purpose, reigniting passions, and crafting a fulfilling life beyond the classroom—all while enjoying your favorite cup of tea or coffee.

What You'll Get:

✶ A supportive community of fellow retired educators who understand your journey

✶ Meaningful discussions on life after teaching, including purpose, passions, and personal growth

✶ Inspiration and encouragement to create a vibrant, fulfilling next chapter

✶ A chance to share and learn from others' experiences in a relaxed and friendly setting

Come as you are, bring your favorite drink, and let's chat about making retirement your most rewarding chapter yet!

Sign up today and be part of this wonderful community.

www.refiredontretire.com/sip-chat

www.ingramcontent.com/pod-product-compliance
Lightning Source LLC
Chambersburg PA
CBHW072159070526
44585CB00015B/1222